CONTENTS

ACKNOWLEDGEMENTS

First up, the idea for this book came from Alan Powell. I now owe him numerous pints, which, I know, he will not decline.

Thanks go also to Martin Ellis, for his belief in the project and his encouragement.

Countless reliable sources have been used in the compilation of this book, including hundreds of websites. These include official Government sites in various countries. For UK information, the excellent parliament.uk has been invaluable. The author would also like to particularly acknowledge the following:

bbc.co.uk · britannica.com · cia.gov/the-world-factbook
constitutioncenter.org · electoral-reform.org.uk
electoralcommission.org.uk · european-union.europa.eu
firstladies.org · govinfo.gov · hansardsociety.org.uk
historyofparliamentonline.org · house.gov
instituteforgovernment.org.uk · nato.int · nps.gov · oed.com
oxforddnb.com · senate.gov · theyworkforyou.com
ukwhoswho.com · un.org · usa.gov · whitehouse.gov
whitehousehistory.org

Information on *Rotten Boroughs* (p. 35) was sourced from:
The History of Parliament: the House of Commons 1820-1832,
ed. DR Fisher, 2009

Finally, this book is for Jacquie, Chris and Andy, the political nerds with whom I share my life.

POLITICS IN THE UK

THE UK PARLIAMENT

The UK Parliament, based in Westminster, is divided into three branches.

The Crown
The Monarch, who has a constitutional, though largely ceremonial, role in opening and dissolving Parliament, appointing Governments and Prime Ministers, and providing assent for legislation.

The House of Commons
Publicly elected with 650 representatives known as Members of Parliament (MPs). The political party with the most MPs usually forms the Government, headed by the Prime Minister.

The House of Lords
Membership is not elected but is a combination of archbishops, bishops, hereditary peers, and life peers and peeresses. Around 800 members are currently eligible to join in the work of the House. The House works independently of the House of Commons and reviews and amends laws passed to it from the House of Commons.

THE OFFICIAL RESIDENCE OF
THE UK PRIME MINISTER

10 Downing Street, Westminster, London SW1A 2AA.

PRIME MINISTERS OF THE UNITED KINGDOM

1721	Robert Walpole	*W*
1742	Spencer Compton	*W*
1743	Henry Pelham	*W*
1754	Thomas Pelham-Holles	*W*
1756	William Cavendish	*W*
1757	Thomas Pelham-Holles	*W*
1762	John Stuart	*T*
1763	George Grenville	*W*
1765	Charles Watson-Wentworth	*W*
1766	William Pitt (the Elder)	*W*
1768	Augustus Fitzroy	*W*
1770	Frederick North	*T*
1782	Charles Watson-Wentworth	*W*
1782	W Petty-Fitzmaurice	*W*
1783	W Cavendish-Bentinck	*Co*
1783	William Pitt (the Younger)	*T*
1801	Henry Addington	*T*
1804	William Pitt (the Younger)	*T*
1806	William Grenville	*Co*
1807	W Cavendish-Bentinck	*T*
1809	Spencer Perceval	*T*
1812	Robert Jenkinson	*T*
1827	George Canning	*Co*
1827	Frederick Robinson	*T*
1828	Arthur Wellesley	*T*
1830	Charles Grey	*W*
1834	William Lamb	*W*
1834	Arthur Wellesley	*T*
1834	Robert Peel	*T*
1835	William Lamb	*W*
1841	Robert Peel	*C*
1846	John Russell	*W*
1852	Edward Smith Stanley	*C*
1852	George Hamilton-Gordon	*Co*
1855	Henry John Temple	*Lib*
1858	Edward Smith Stanley	*C*
1859	Henry John Temple	*Lib*
1865	John Russell	*Lib*
1866	Edward Smith Stanley	*C*
1868	Benjamin Disraeli	*C*
1868	William Gladstone	*Lib*
1874	Benjamin Disraeli	*C*
1880	William Gladstone	*Lib*
1885	Robert Gascoyne-Cecil	*C*
1886	William Gladstone	*Lib*
1886	Robert Gascoyne-Cecil	*C*
1892	William Gladstone	*Lib*
1894	Archibald Primrose	*Lib*
1895	Robert Gascoyne-Cecil	*C*
1902	Arthur Balfour	*C*
1905	H Campbell-Bannerman	*Lib*
1908	Herbert Asquith	*Lib/Co*
1916	David Lloyd George	*Co*
1922	Andrew Bonar Law	*C*
1923	Stanley Baldwin	*C*
1924	Ramsay MacDonald	*Lab*
1924	Stanley Baldwin	*C*
1929	Ramsay MacDonald	*Lab/Co*
1935	Stanley Baldwin	*Co*
1937	Neville Chamberlain	*Co*
1940	Winston Churchill	*Co*
1945	Clement Attlee	*Lab*
1951	Winston Churchill	*C*
1955	Anthony Eden	*C*
1957	Harold Macmillan	*C*
1963	Alec Douglas-Home	*C*
1964	Harold Wilson	*Lab*
1970	Edward Heath	*C*
1974	Harold Wilson	*Lab*
1976	James Callaghan	*Lab*
1979	Margaret Thatcher	*C*
1990	John Major	*C*
1997	Tony Blair	*Lab*
2007	Gordon Brown	*Lab*
2010	David Cameron	*C*
2016	Theresa May	*C*
2019	Boris Johnson	*C*
2022	Liz Truss	*C*

SOME THINGS NOT ALLOWED IN THE CHAMBER OF THE HOUSE OF COMMONS

Accompanying children (except to pass through to division lobbies)
Clapping (unless spontaneous and non-partisan)
Eating or drinking (except water or for health reasons)
Electronic devices which make a noise
Filming or taking photographs
Jeans, T-shirts, sandals and trainers
Laptops
Large briefcases
Making audio recordings
Prominent branding
Reading of newspapers
Smoking
Taking phone calls or listening to voicemail
Wearing of medals or uniforms

THE PALACE OF WESTMINSTER

The UK Parliament meets at the Palace of Westminster in London, a building with origins that date back to a royal palace built on the banks of the River Thames by King Canute in the 11th century. A new structure was completed soon after by one of his successors, Edward the Confessor, and then expanded by Kings William I and William II, the latter adding Westminster Hall that remains to this day.

Various prototype Parliaments convened at the Palace over the centuries until 1512, when its time as a royal residence ended after a fire and Parliament was able to firmly establish itself on the premises – the Commons meeting in St Stephen's Chapel and the Lords resident in a hall known as the Queen's Chamber.

Another catastrophic fire, in 1834, saw the destruction of most of the Palace complex, leading to its reconstruction in Gothic Revival style by 1860 by the architects Charles Barry and Augustus Pugin.

Further damage occurred as the result of an air raid in the Second World War, when the Chamber of the House of Commons was destroyed by fire.

Today's Palace, along with nearby Westminster Abbey, is a designated UNESCO World Heritage Site.

THE PASSAGE OF A BILL

A guide to how a Bill (a draft proposal) becomes law in the UK Parliament.

First Reading (Commons)
The short title of the Bill is read in the House of Commons. Normally a formality, with no debate.

Second Reading (Commons)
Debate on the general principles of the Bill, opened by a Government minister or other MP responsible for the Bill. Vote on whether it proceeds to the next stage.

Committee Stage (Commons)
Full scrutiny by a Public Bill Committee of 17 MPs, appointed by the Selection Committee (a committee of MPs that nominates Members to serve on various bodies). Evidence from interested parties and experts from outside Parliament can be taken; clauses may be changed/removed; MPs' amendments may be included. The Committee normally has a majority of MPs from the governing party.

Report Stage (Commons)
Debate allowing MPs to discuss and propose further amendments.

Third Reading (Commons)
Debate and vote on the Bill with no further amendments allowed. If approved, the Bill progresses to the House of Lords.

First Reading (Lords)
Normally a formality, as in the House of Commons.

Second Reading (Lords)
Debate on the key issues of the Bill.

Committee Stage (Lords)
Full scrutiny with any member of the House allowed to participate.

Report Stage (Lords)
Debate allowing Members to discuss the Bill and also propose further amendments.

Third Reading (Lords)
Debate allowing further amendments.

Consideration of Amendments
The Bill returns to the House of Commons for consideration of amendments made in the House of Lords. Any dispute may see the Bill 'ping pong' between the two Houses until agreement is reached. If no agreement is possible, the Bill falls, but the House of Commons, in some instances, can enforce its will.

Royal Assent
Once the Bill is agreed by the two Houses, it receives Royal Assent and becomes an Act of Parliament, with the proposals becoming law.

Note: A similar process (reversed) applies for Bills proposed by the House of Lords.

THE PRIME MINISTER

The Prime Minister is the head of the UK Government and usually the leader of the largest party in the House of Commons. Appointed by the Monarch, the Prime Minister selects other members of the Cabinet. Robert Walpole became the first acknowledged Prime Minister in 1721, when the Monarch (King George I) stopped chairing meetings of his ministers and effectively handed more power to the leader of the Government. However, the description 'Prime Minister' was initially used as a term of abuse, suggesting that the holder had arrogantly pushed himself above others, and was probably borrowed from France. The title became official in 1905 when it was bestowed upon Henry Campbell-Bannerman. The Prime Minister is usually also the First Lord of the Treasury, which entitles the holder to move into 10 Downing Street, the First Lord of the Treasury's official residence.

HOW MUCH DO THEY EARN?

The annual salary of a UK Member of Parliament in 2022–23 was £84,144 with the following office holders receiving this salary topped up as shown.*

Position	£
Prime Minister	75,440
Cabinet Minister	67,505
Minister of State	31,680
Parliamentary Under-Secretary of State	22,475
Select Committee Chair	16,422
Leader of the Opposition	65,181

* MPs are also entitled to various expenses to cover office, staffing and accommodation costs.

PARLIAMENTARY SESSIONS

A Parliamentary session generally lasts one year, usually beginning and ending in spring. Breaks in each session are known as recesses and cover holiday periods such as Christmas, Easter and summer, plus a few weeks in the early autumn when the party conferences are held. The Government may request a recall of Parliament during a recess if there is business of national importance to discuss, with the final decision made by The Speaker.

THE YOUNGEST AND OLDEST PRIME MINISTERS

Prime Minister	Age*
Youngest	
1 ....William Pitt (the Younger)	24 years 205 days
2 ....Augustus Fitzroy	33 years 16 days
3 ....Charles Watson-Wentworth	35 years 61 days
4 ....William Cavendish	36 years 168 days†
5 ....Frederick North	37 years 290 days
6 ....Robert Jenkinson	42 years 1 day
7 ....David Cameron	43 years 214 days
8 ....Henry Addington	43 years 291 days
9 ....Tony Blair	43 years 361 days
10 ......Robert Walpole	44 years 220 days
Oldest	
46 ......Benjamin Disraeli	63 years 68 days
47 ......James Callaghan	64 years 9 days
48 ......Andrew Bonar Law	64 years 37 days
49 ......Winston Churchill	65 years 162 days
50 ......Charles Grey	66 years 254 days
51 ......Neville Chamberlain	68 years 71 days
52 ......Spencer Compton	c.68–69 years‡
53 ......George Hamilton-Gordon	68 years 326 days
54 ......Henry Campbell-Bannerman	69 years 89 days
55 ......Henry John Temple	70 years 109 days

* When taking office. † Exact age uncertain; baptism date used.
‡ Date of birth unknown, presumed to be c.1674.

ELECTION THURSDAYS

A general election may be called for any day of the week, but, since 1935, all general elections have been held on a Thursday, although there is no obvious reason why this has become the norm. Theories suggest that it is because – Thursday traditionally being a market day – people will be out and about anyway and therefore more likely to vote. There's also the idea that it may be because weekends are best avoided so that voters are not unduly swayed by the conflicting attractions of the pub and the church (and the powerful opinions and persuasions encountered in both environments).

THE PMQS PROCEDURE

Prime Minister's Question Time (PMQs) takes place on Wednesdays when Parliament is in session. The process begins at 12 noon and lasts roughly 30 minutes. Although often a rowdy and chaotic occasion, PMQs is not a free-for-all, with the procedure outlined below strictly followed by the Speaker.

1 Routine question from an MP – from the Government or an Opposition party – regarding the Prime Minister's engagements. This being an 'open question', it can be followed up by a supplementary question on any topic, the text of which is not pre-published and, therefore in theory, is unknown to the Prime Minister. Alternatively, what are known as 'substantive' questions may be asked and these are published in advance.

2 Questions from the Leader of the Opposition: maximum of six, which may be asked consecutively or broken up into smaller batches.*

3 Questions from the leader of the third-largest party: maximum of two.

4 Questions from other MPs who are pre-selected via a ballot. They are called in turn by the Speaker who alternates questions between the Government and Opposition benches. Additional questions come from MPs who catch the Speaker's attention by 'bobbing' (standing up as the Prime Minister concludes an answer to a previous question).

* A Government MP's question may sometimes precede questions from the Leader of the Opposition and the leader of the third-largest party, to ensure alternating Government-Opposition questions.

ELECTORAL FAILURES OF NIGEL FARAGE

Nigel Farage has tried – and failed – to win a seat in Parliament seven times.

Year	Constituency	Party	Votes/Share	Pos
1994	Eastleigh (BE)	UKIP	952/1.7%	4th
1997	Salisbury (GE)	UKIP	3,332/5.7%	4th
2001	Bexhill & Battle (GE)	UKIP	3,474/7.8%	4th (last)
2005	South Thanet (GE)	UKIP	2,079/5%	4th
2006	Bromley & Chislehurst (BE)	UKIP	2,347/8.1%	3rd
2010	Buckingham (GE)	UKIP	8,401/17.4%	3rd
2015	South Thanet (GE)	UKIP	16,026/32.4%	2nd

THE SPEAKER OF THE HOUSE OF COMMONS

The Speaker – assisted by three Deputy Speakers – is the person who chairs the proceedings of the House of Commons, maintaining order, calling MPs to speak and ruling which amendments may be made to bills, as well as taking responsibility for the upkeep and security of the buildings of the House.

The holder of the position is an MP who has been elected by fellow MPs in a secret ballot presided over by the Father of the House.

Although, during the tenure of the position, the Speaker adopts a politically impartial position and resigns party membership, they remain a constituency MP and deal with constituent business just like other MPs.

Voting for the election of Speaker may take several rounds but, once the winner has been declared, they are ritually 'dragged' from their place on the Commons benches and installed in the Speaker's chair – a charade that probably stems from the reluctance of certain MPs to take on the role of Speaker when it was a dangerous position – a number of holders of the office literally lost their heads after fulfilling their duty of 'speaking' to the Monarch on behalf of the Commons.

In any general election that occurs during their tenure, it is tradition for the Speaker to run for election as an MP unopposed by all the major parties, but the Speaker does then need to be re-elected to the role once Parliament resumes its work. A simple motion to confirm this, rather than a secret ballot, is usually the mechanism used in such circumstances.

The first officially recorded Speaker was Sir Thomas Hungerford, a close associate of John O' Gaunt, who was appointed to the role in 1377.

Recent Speakers of the House of Commons

1857	Evelyn Denison *W*	1959	Harry Hylton-Foster *C*
1872	Henry Bland *Lib*	1965	Horace King *Lab*
1884	Arthur Peel *Lib*	1971	Selwyn Lloyd *C*
1895	William Court Gully *Lib*	1976	George Thomas *Lab*
1905	James Lowther *C*	1983	Bernard Weatherill *C*
1921	John Henry Whitley *Lib*	1992	Betty Boothroyd *Lab*
1928	Edward Fitzroy *C*	2000	Michael Martin *Lab*
1943	Douglas Clifton Brown *C*	2009	John Bercow *C*
1951	William Morrison *C*	2019	Lindsay Hoyle *Lab*

THE OATH OF ALLEGIANCE

On entering Parliament, or returning to Parliament after an election, MPs and Lords swear an oath of allegiance to the Crown at the Table of the House, using the following wording:

I (name) swear by Almighty God* that I will be faithful and bear true allegiance to Her/His Majesty (name of Monarch), her/his heirs and successors, according to law. So help me God.

A sacred text is held, kissed or kept close at hand at the same time. After the oath has been spoken in English, it may be repeated in Welsh, Scottish Gaelic or Cornish. In place of an oath, MPs may make a solemn affirmation, using the following wording:

I (name) do solemnly, sincerely, and truly declare and affirm, that I will be faithful and bear true allegiance to Her/His Majesty (name of Monarch), her/his heirs and successors, according to law.

Failure to swear an oath or make a solemn affirmation means that MPs are not allowed to take their seats, speak in debates or receive a salary. A fine of £500 may also be levied on them and their seat may be declared vacant.

* The words 'by Almighty God' may be omitted if preferred.

SWING WHEN YOU'RE WINNING

The advantage that television has over radio is, of course, visual, and when it comes to coverage of elections there have been various brave attempts to exert that advantage, most notably with the creation of the Swingometer in 1955. The brainchild of political scientist David Butler, who developed the concept of 'swing' to show the movement of support between parties several years earlier, the Swingometer was devised as a kind of speedometer showing percentage points of support rather than miles per hour and was brought to life on screen by the Bristol university academic Stephen Milne. That first device was rather rudimental and its appearance was only fleeting but, from the 1959 general election, the Swingometer became a mainstay of the BBC's election coverage, with presenters such as Butler himself, Bob Mackenzie, Peter Snow and Jeremy Vine calculating the likely size of party majorities with the use of its fluctuating needle as the results rolled in.

CROSSBENCHERS

In the House of Lords, independent or neutral members who adopt no party affiliation are known as Crossbench Peers because the seats they occupy are set out across the Chamber, at right angles to the party benches.

RECENT LEADERS OF THE CONSERVATIVE PARTY

1940	Winston Churchill	1997	William Hague
1955	Anthony Eden	2001	Iain Duncan Smith
1957	Harold Macmillan	2003	Michael Howard
1963	Alec Douglas-Home	2005	David Cameron
1965	Edward Heath	2016	Theresa May
1975	Margaret Thatcher	2019	Boris Johnson
1990	John Major	2022	Liz Truss

PRIVATE MEMBERS' BILLS

A Private Members' Bill is a bill that is put forward by a backbench MP, rather than the Government or Opposition, and can be introduced in three ways.

The first, and most likely to be successful, way is via what is known as the Ballot, in which the names of all MPs wishing to propose a bill are drawn at random early in a new Parliamentary session. Those drawn first have priority over the time available for such bills in the House of Commons.

The second way is via the Ten Minute Rule Bill, which allows MPs to put forward a bill and speak for no more than ten minutes on it.

The final way is the Presentation Bill, in which a bill is put forward but the MP does not actually speak on the subject.

Private Members' Bills are usually considered on Fridays but, because little time is allocated for these bills to pass through all the stages required, most fail to make it into law. However, MPs know that the process of putting forward such a bill does at least generate publicity around a particular issue.

Note: Members of the House of Lords can also put forward Private Members' Bills (following a slightly different procedure), which, if successful, will pass to the House of Commons for the consideration of MPs.

THE BUDGET

The Budget is the Government's annual financial statement to the country and is formally delivered by the Chancellor of the Exchequer to the House of Commons in what amounts to one of Parliament's great showpiece occasions.

In recent years, the Budget has been presented at lunchtime on a Wednesday in the autumn, but in the past it has also been presented in the spring, and could take place on another day of the week.

The name Budget is derived from the French for 'little bag', a reference to a bag in which the financial documents were once carried to the House for the speech. These days, a Budget box, rather than a bag, is used and the Chancellor makes a great play of holding this up for the media before leaving Downing Street for the Commons, although the box itself has been replaced a number of times over the decades. Occasionally, one of the older boxes is retrieved for the spectacle.

The Budget speech usually opens with details of the state of the economy and the country's finances, together with forecasts of future trends prepared by the Office for Budget Responsibility. It goes on to explain any new taxes or financial initiatives that are planned for the next year or forthcoming years.

Tradition and precedent dictate that the immediate Opposition response to the speech is given not by the Shadow Chancellor but by the Leader of the Opposition who has the unenviable task of providing critical analysis without (normally) having seen or heard the contents of the Budget speech in advance.

The Budget gains approval from the House via the Finance Bill, which is voted on four days after the speech, following much debate and after MPs have had the opportunity to scrutinise all the supporting financial data published by the Treasury in the so-called *Red Book* (named after the colour of its cover). The Bill puts into action the proposals in the Budget. Some taxes – such as excise duties on tobacco or car fuel – are customarily approved as soon as the Chancellor has completed the presentation, to allow their introduction within hours.

Although the House of Lords studies and debates the Finance Bill, it does not amend it – the Lords defer to the primacy of the House of Commons when it comes to matters of taxation and expenditure.

The longest Budget speech was delivered by William Gladstone in 1853 (4 hours 45 minutes) and the shortest by Benjamin Disraeli in 1867 (45 minutes).

UNPARLIAMENTARY LANGUAGE

Standards of politeness in the House of Commons Chamber are enforced by the Speaker. In the case of 'unparliamentary language' being used – often to attack or defame an opposing member – the Speaker will ask for the comment to be withdrawn. A refusal to do so can lead to disciplinary measures, including the Member being 'named' and possibly expelled from the Chamber. Words that have been known to provoke the Speaker include:

bastard · blackguard · bollocks · coward · deliberately deceptive
dishonest · dodgy · drunk · falsehoods · git · guttersnipe · hooligan
hypocrite · liar · racist · rat · squirt · stoolpigeon · swine · traitor · wart

NOBLE TITLES OF BRITISH PRIME MINISTERS WHILE IN OFFICE

Spencer Compton	1st Earl of Wilmington
Thomas Pelham-Holles	1st Duke of Newcastle
William Cavendish	4th Duke of Devonshire
John Stuart	3rd Earl of Bute
Charles Watson-Wentworth	2nd Marquess of Rockingham
William Pitt (the Elder)	1st Earl of Chatham
Augustus Fitzroy	3rd Duke of Grafton
Frederick North	Lord North
William Petty-Fitzmaurice	2nd Earl of Shelburne
William Cavendish-Bentinck	3rd Duke of Portland
William Grenville	1st Baron Grenville
Robert Jenkinson	2nd Earl of Liverpool
Frederick Robinson	1st Viscount Goderich
Arthur Wellesley	1st Duke of Wellington
Charles Grey	2nd Earl Grey
William Lamb	2nd Viscount Melbourne
Robert Peel	2nd Baronet Peel
John Russell	1st Earl Russell
Edward Smith Stanley	14th Earl of Derby
George Hamilton-Gordon	4th Earl of Aberdeen
Henry John Temple	3rd Viscount Palmerston
Benjamin Disraeli	Earl of Beaconsfield
Robert Gascoyne-Cecil	3rd Marquess of Salisbury
Archibald Primrose	5th Earl of Rosebery

NOBLE TITLES OF BRITISH PRIME MINISTERS AFTER LEAVING OFFICE

Robert Walpole	1st Earl of Orford
Frederick North	2nd Earl of Guilford
William Petty-Fitzmaurice	1st Marquess of Lansdowne
Henry Addington	1st Viscount Sidmouth
Frederick Robinson	1st Earl of Ripon
Arthur Balfour	1st Earl of Balfour
Herbert Asquith	1st Earl of Oxford and Asquith
David Lloyd George	1st Earl Lloyd-George of Dwyfor
Stanley Baldwin	1st Earl Baldwin of Bewdley
Clement Attlee	1st Earl Attlee of Walthamstow
Anthony Eden	1st Earl of Avon
Harold Macmillan	1st Earl of Stockton
Alec Douglas-Home	Baron Home of the Hirsel
Harold Wilson	Baron Wilson of Rievaulx
James Callaghan	Baron Callaghan of Cardiff
Margaret Thatcher	Baroness Thatcher of Kesteven

RETURNING OFFICERS, RECOUNTS AND DEAD HEATS

The (Acting) Returning Officer is a local authority official who is appointed to conduct an election. The role involves anything from publishing notice of the election to printing ballot papers and publishing the result. The duties of the Returning Officer after the votes have been counted are as follows.

1 The Returning Officer confirms that the number of votes attracted by each candidate is correct and informs the candidates and their election agents accordingly. At this stage, any candidate may request a recount, but the Returning Officer has the final say on this.

2 Once all candidates agree that the result may be declared, the public announcement is made.

3 Should two or more candidates in a Parliamentary election jointly top the poll with the same number of votes, the winner of the election is decided by lot, with the Returning Officer deciding how this should be conducted, which could be as simply as tossing a coin or, slightly more appropriately perhaps, by placing marked pieces of paper in an empty ballot box and drawing out the winner unseen.

SOME IMPORTANT PARLIAMENTARY OFFICIALS

Black Rod

The Lady or Gentleman Usher of the Black Rod – Black Rod for short – is the senior official responsible for controlling access to the House of Lords and for maintaining order in the Lords Chamber. Black Rod also takes charge of ceremonial occasions, assisted by a deputy known as the Yeoman Usher of the Black Rod. As part of the State Opening of Parliament, Black Rod is sent to the House of Commons to summon MPs to the House of Lords to hear the Monarch's Speech. On arrival, it is customary for the doors of the House to be slammed shut as a bold show of the Commons' independence, requiring Black Rod to smite the door three times with the ceremonial ebony rod for it to reopen. The first Lady Usher of the Black Rod, Sarah Clarke, was appointed in 2017 and assumed her duties in 2018.

Clerk of the House of Commons

A politically-impartial officer appointed by the Crown who records all decisions taken by the House from a seat at the House Table, close to The Speaker's chair, traditionally attired in wig and silk gown. The Clerk also serves as the principal adviser to the House on constitutional issues and procedure, and has corporate responsibilities for both the budget and the administration of the House.

Clerk of the Parliaments

The most senior House of Lords official, appointed by the Crown and responsible for employing staff, keeping official records, delivering financial accounts and offering advice on procedure.

Serjeant at Arms

A sort of House of Commons security guard – complete with sword and uniform – appointed by the Crown, whose duties include keeping order and escorting MPs from the House when they have been excluded by the Speaker. The Serjeant at Arms ceremonially carries the mace into the House during the Speaker's procession before each sitting and also has responsibility for committee rooms and public galleries.

ANOTHER PLACE

It is a strange convention of Parliament – dating from the 19th century – that Members of the House of Commons and the House of Lords do not actually refer to each others' House by name when speaking in the Chambers but instead use the terminology 'another place' or 'the other place'.

COMMON ABBREVIATIONS IN UK POLITICS

APPG... All-Party Parliamentary Group
AS...Aelodau o'r Senedd (Member of Senedd, Wales)
BEIS ....Department for Business, Energy & Industrial Strategy
CO.. Cabinet Office
DCMS....................................Department for Digital, Culture, Media & Sport
Defra...............................Department for Environment, Food & Rural Affairs
DexEU ....Department for Exiting the European Union*
DfE... Department for Education
DFID..Department for International Development*
DHSC ....Department for Health and Social Care
DIT ....Department for International Trade
DLUHC ....Department for Levelling Up, Housing & Communities†
DWP...Department for Work and Pensions
EDM .... Early Day Motion
FCDO ....Foreign, Commonwealth & Development Office‡
HMRC .... Her/His Majesty's Revenue and Customs
HMT..Her/His Majesty's Treasury
HO ....Home Office
IPSA.....................................Independent Parliamentary Standards Authority
MHCLG .... Ministry of Housing, Communities & Local Government*
MLA ....Member of the Legislative Assembly (Northern Ireland)
MoD.. Ministry of Defence
MoJ .... Ministry of Justice
MP ....Member of Parliament
MS...Member of Senedd (Wales)
MSP ....Member of Scottish Parliament
NAO...National Audit Office
OBR .... Office for Budget Responsibility
PAC.. Public Accounts Committee
PC .... Privy Council
PLP... Parliamentary Labour Party
PM ....Prime Minister
PMB... Private Members' Bill
PPS.. Parliamentary Private Secretary
Quango.......................Quasi Autonomous Non Governmental Organisation

* Department now closed.
† Formerly Ministry of Housing, Communities & Local Government.
‡ Formerly Foreign and Commonwealth Office (FCO).

A BREXIT TIMELINE

1 January 1973 .... The UK joins the EEC (which becomes the EU in 1993).

5 June 1975 .... In a referendum held on continued membership of the EEC, the UK votes to stay in (67.2%/32.8%).

12 September 2006.. Nigel Farage becomes leader of the UK Independence Party and later leads it to success in European and some UK elections on a strident platform of leaving the EU.

23 January 2013 ..... Prime Minister David Cameron pledges an 'in/out' referendum on EU membership in a bid to heal divisions within the Conservative Party and country.

23 June 2016 .... In the referendum, the UK votes to leave the EU (51.9%/48.1%). Cameron resigns the next day.

13 July 2016 .... Theresa May becomes Prime Minister. Subsequent discussions with the EU over new arrangements for trade stumble over the issue of Northern Ireland's open border with the Republic of Ireland. May's proposed 'backstop' commits the UK to remaining in a customs union with the EU until agreement is reached on the Irish border issue, but this is later rejected by MPs.

29 March 2017 .... May formally notifies the EU of the UK's decision to leave and a two-year countdown to departure begins.

8 June 2017 .... May loses her Government majority in a general election called in a bid to strengthen her negotiating hand.

21 March 2019 .... The EU agrees the first of what will be three extensions to the deadline for the UK's departure.

7 June 2019 .... May resigns as Prime Minister.

24 July 2019 .... Boris Johnson becomes Prime Minister and commits to scrapping the idea of a backstop.

12 December 2019.. A general election is held to break the stalemate in the House of Commons. Johnson, campaigning on a slogan of 'Get Brexit Done', wins an 80-seat majority for the Conservative Party.

24 December 2019.. A deal is reached between the EU and the UK. To resolve the Ireland impasse, Johnson agrees that goods will be subject to customs checks between the British mainland and Northern Ireland (the 'Northern Ireland Protocol').

31 January 2020 ..... The UK officially leaves the EU. However, an agreed transition period, ending on 31 December 2020, means the UK will continue to follow EU rules while new arrangements are gradually put in place.

THE FASTEST/SLOWEST CONSTITUENCY COUNTS

Constituency	Time Declared
Fastest	
1 ....Newcastle upon Tyne Central	23:27
2 ....Houghton & Sunderland South	23:29
3 ....Blyth Valley	23:32
4 ....Newcastle upon Tyne East	00:05
5 ....Sunderland Central	00:08
6 ....Middlesbrough	00:25
7 ....North Swindon	00:30
8 ....Washington & Sunderland West	00:41
9 ....Newcastle upon Tyne North	00:46
10 ......Halton	00:47
Slowest	
641 ....Orkney & Shetland	06:01
642 ....Croydon North	06:02
643 ....Cheltenham	06:29
644 ....Croydon South	06:33
645 ....Horsham	06:35
646 ....Torridge & West Devon	06:56
647 ....Fermanagh & South Tyrone	06:59
648 ....South Northamptonshire	07:13
649 ....Arundel & South Downs	08:09
650 ....St Ives	14:52

Note: 2019 General Election. Polls closed at 22:00.

THE MANSION HOUSE SPEECH

One of British politics' grand annual set pieces is the Mansion House Speech, delivered each June by the Chancellor of the Exchequer. The Chancellor traditionally uses this occasion to inform City bankers and merchants about the Government's financial strategies and its overall view of the economy, and is often an occasion for announcing new policies. The venue, the Mansion House, is the official home of the Lord Mayor of London and the event is a black tie affair, which the new Chancellor Gordon Brown famously rebelled against in 1997, when he insisted on addressing the audience in what was described as his 'working clothes' – a lounge suit.

PRAYING FOR A SEAT

Daily sittings in Parliament begin with prayers, led usually by the Speaker's Chaplain in the Commons and a senior bishop in the Lords. MPs stand for the service and turn to face the wall behind them – possibly a throwback to the days when wearing a sword might make it difficult to kneel. The wording of the prayer for the Commons is generally as follows:

Lord, the God of righteousness and truth, grant to our Queen/King and her/his government, to Members of Parliament and all in positions of responsibility, the guidance of your Spirit. May they never lead the nation wrongly through love of power, desire to please, or unworthy ideals but laying aside all private interests and prejudices keep in mind their responsibility to seek to improve the condition of all mankind; so may your kingdom come and your name be hallowed. Amen.

MPs can book a place for prayers by placing a green prayer card on a seat. As this then allows them to use that seat for the rest of the day, this procedure is often used to secure a place for a major event later in the day.

KEEPING AN EYE ON THE BOOKS

The Government's handling of the country's finances is monitored and scrutinised by the following bodies that each have independent functions.

National Audit Office (NAO)
The public spending watchdog, headed by the Comptroller and Auditor General who certifies the accounts of all the Government's departments and delivers reports to Parliament on whether resources have been allocated wisely and economically.

Public Accounts Committee (PAC)
A committee of MPs, informed by the NAO, who monitor and question the Government's spending but focusing only on how money has been spent and not why it has been spent (i.e. execution rather than policy).

Office for Budget Responsibility (OBR)
An independent body that analyses the Government's fiscal policy and performance, producing economic forecasts, assessing performance against fiscal targets, analysing the long-term sustainability of the public finances, evaluating fiscal risks and scrutinising tax and welfare spending plans.

OXBRIDGE PRIME MINISTERS

Oxford

Prime Minister	College	Prime Minister	College
Spencer Compton	Trinity	R Gascoyne-Cecil	Christ Church
Henry Pelham	Hart Hall*	Archibald Primrose	Christ Church
George Grenville	Christ Church	Herbert Asquith	Balliol
William Pitt (the Elder)	Trinity	Clement Attlee	University College
Frederick North	Trinity	Anthony Eden	Christ Church
W Petty-Fitzmaurice	Christ Church	Harold Macmillan	Balliol
W Cavendish-Bentinck	Christ Church	A Douglas-Home	Christ Church
Henry Addington	Brasenose	Harold Wilson	Jesus
William Grenville	Christ Church	Edward Heath	Balliol
Robert Jenkinson	Christ Church	Margaret Thatcher	Somerville
George Canning	Christ Church	Tony Blair	St John's
Robert Peel	Christ Church	David Cameron	Brasenose
John Russell	Christ Church	Theresa May	St Hugh's
William Gladstone	Christ Church	Boris Johnson	Balliol
		Liz Truss	Merton

Cambridge

Prime Minister	College	Prime Minister	College
Robert Walpole	King's	William Lamb	Trinity
Thomas Pelham-Holles	Clare	George Hamilton-Gordon	St John's
Augustus Fitzroy	Peterhouse	Henry John Temple	St John's
W Pitt (the Younger)	Pembroke	Arthur Balfour	Trinity
Spencer Perceval	Trinity	H Campbell-Bannerman	Trinity
Frederick Robinson	St John's	Stanley Baldwin	Trinity
Charles Grey	Trinity		

* Now Hertford College; also Pelham initially studied at King's, Cambridge.

SECRETARIES AND MINISTERS

In the hierarchy of Government, secretaries of state are Cabinet ministers with overall responsibility for key departments, such as foreign affairs, home affairs, education, business, defence, transport and health. Beneath them sit ministers of state (commonly known just as 'ministers') who take charge of policy within departments, and below them are what are known as parliamentary under-secretaries of state (or simply 'under-secretaries').

A HISTORY OF UK REFERENDUMS

Year	Area	Question	Yes/No	Turnout
1973	N Ireland	Do you want N Ireland to remain part of the United Kingdom?	98.9/1.1	58.7
1975	UK	Do you think that the UK should stay in the European Community (the Common Market)?	67.2/32.8	64.0
1979	Scotland	Do you want the provisions of the Scotland Act 1978 to be put into effect?	51.6/48.4	63.6*
	Wales	Do you want the provisions of the Wales Act 1978 to be put into effect?	20.3/79.7	58.8
1997	Scotland	I agree/do not agree that there should be a Scottish Parliament.	74.3/25.7	60.2
	Scotland	I agree/do not agree that a Scottish Parliament should have tax-varying powers.	63.5/36.55	60.2
	Wales	I agree/do not agree that there should be a Welsh Assembly.	50.3/49.7	50.1
1998	London	Are you in favour of the Government's proposals for a Greater London Authority, made up of an elected mayor and a separately elected assembly?	72.0/28.0	34.0
	N Ireland	Do you support the Agreement reached at the Multi-Party Talks in N Ireland and set out in Command Paper 3883?	71.1/28.9	81.0
2004	NE England	Should there be an elected assembly for the North East region?	22.1/77.9	47.1
2011	Wales	Do you want the Assembly now to be able to make laws on all matters in the 20 subject areas it has powers for?	63.5/36.5	35.6
	UK	At present, the UK uses the 'first past the post' system to elect MPs to the House of Commons. Should the 'alternative vote' system be used instead?	32.1/67.9	42.2
2014	Scotland	Should Scotland be an independent country?	44.7/55.3	84.6
2016	UK	Should the UK remain a member of the European Union or leave the European Union?	48.1/51.9	72.2

* Less than 40 per cent of the electorate voted 'yes' so devolution did not proceed.

SOME MARRIED MPS IN RECENT YEARS

Virginia Bottomley and Peter Bottomley C
Jenny Chapman and Nick Smith *Lab*
Yvette Cooper and Ed Balls *Lab*
Caroline Dinenage and Mark Lancaster C
Gwyneth Dunwoody and John Dunwoody *Lab*
Harriet Harman and Jack Dromey *Lab*
Andrea Jenkyns and Jack Lopresti C
Ann Keen and Alan Keen *Lab*
Anne Kerr and Russell Kerr *Lab*
Julie Kirkbride and Andrew MacKay C
Esther McVey and Philip Davies C
Bridget Prentice and Gordon Prentice *Lab*
Ellie Reeves and John Cryer *Lab*
Joan Ruddock and Frank Doran *Lab*
Alison Seabeck and Nick Raynsford *Lab*
Jo Swinson and Duncan Hames *LD*
Ann Winterton and Nicholas Winterton C

Note: Both partners serving MPs while married. Not surprisingly, all the above
married couples are/were members of the same political party.

BUDGET PURDAH

Derived from a mixed Persian-Urdu word meaning 'curtain', and originally
referring to the privacy accorded to Muslim and Hindu women behind such
a screen, purdah has evolved into a general term for isolation or secrecy
and, in political terms, has been particularly associated with the post of
Chancellor of the Exchequer. Traditionally, as the Budget announcement
drew near, the Chancellor would retreat into purdah, a period during which
he would decline to comment on what the Budget might entail. This was
seen as a precaution against market-sensitive information being released. It
was also a matter of honour and of courtesy to the House of Commons.
Famously, the Labour Chancellor Hugh Dalton resigned his position in
1947 after comments he made on his way into the Chamber for the
announcement found their way into the press before he had completed
his speech. The purdah tradition was abandoned in 1993 and various
Chancellors since have made full use of their new freedom to deliberately
leak suggestions of what the Budget might entail for some political advantage.

CROSSING THE FLOOR

When an MP leaves one party and joins another, the process is often described as 'crossing the floor', a reference to moving from one side of the House of Commons Chamber to another. However, such a visibly dramatic gesture is rarely seen because MPs often defect outside Parliament and simply sit with their new colleagues the next time they enter the Chamber.

RECENT LEADERS OF THE LABOUR PARTY

1935	Clement Attlee	1992	John Smith
1955	Hugh Gaitskell	1994	Tony Blair
1963	Harold Wilson	2007	Gordon Brown
1976	James Callaghan	2010	Ed Miliband
1980	Michael Foot	2015	Jeremy Corbyn
1983	Neil Kinnock	2020	Keir Starmer

PORTCULLIS HOUSE

Offices for many MPs and their staff, as well as a number of conference and meeting rooms, are housed across the road from the Palace of Westminster in Portcullis House, easing the burden on the rather overcrowded historic structure. The modern building, named after the emblem of Parliament, was officially opened in 2001 and is linked by a tunnel to the main complex.

PARLIAMENTARY PRIVATE SECRETARIES

A Parliamentary Private Secretary (PPS) is a backbench MP who has been appointed as an assistant by a minister. The position is unpaid but offers good opportunities for gaining experience and career advancement within Government. The job basically involves providing feedback to the minister about the thoughts and opinions of other backbench MPs and also passing information back the other way. PPSs can often been seen handing notes or civil service documents to ministers from their customary seats immediately behind the front bench. They are not officially members of the Government but are required to support the Government in votes. They are not barred from Commons committee work, although they are expected to recuse themselves from any inquiries relating to their own minister's brief.

SOME ODD PARTY NAMES

Some peculiar party names and candidate descriptions seen in UK elections.

21st Century Independent Foresters
Alfred Chicken
Beer, Baccy and Scratchings*
Blancmange Throwers Party†
Bus-Pass Elvis
Captain Beany of the Bean Party
Church of the Militant Elvis
Corrective Party
Elvis Loves Pets
Fancy Dress Party
Fur Play Party‡
Miss Great Britain Party
Mongolian Barbeque Great Place to Party
Official Acne Party
Official Monster Raving Loony Party
Official News Bunny Party
Re-classify The Sun Newspaper a Comic
Sack Graham Taylor
Save the 2CV

* Originally known as Beer, Baccy and Crumpet until the Electoral Commission declared this to be offensive.

† Candidate was the comedian Pamela Stephenson.

‡ Candidate was one Harry Bear.

THE HOUSE OF COMMONS MACE

At the start of each day when the House of Commons is in session, the mace is carried into the Chamber by the Serjeant at Arms, as part of the Speaker's procession. It is a symbol of royal authority and the Commons cannot meet or pass laws without it. If the House is sitting, the mace is placed on the Table of the House; if the House is in committee, it is placed in brackets fixed beneath the Table. The current mace, which is made of silver gilt and just under five feet long, probably dates back to the reign of King Charles II. In the House of Lords, two maces are used, with one mace carried in with the Lord Speaker and placed on the Woolsack whenever the House is in session.

THE MINISTERIAL CODE

Standards of conduct for Government ministers are laid out in a set of rules and principles known as the *Ministerial Code*, with similar documents issued for the devolved administrations in Scotland, Wales and Northern Ireland. The Code has been in existence since the Second World War or earlier but was only published for the first time in 1992, under John Major, with the title *Questions of Procedure for Ministers*. The present title was adopted under Tony Blair in 1997 and the document is generally updated at the beginning of each new administration. Even though, since 2006, an independent advisor has been appointed to maintain a register of ministers' interests and provide guidance, the Prime Minister remains the supreme arbiter of whether the code has been broken or even whether alleged instances of non-compliance are investigated. In his introduction to the 2019 update of the *Code*, Boris Johnson stressed the following points of ministerial conduct had to be observed:

No bullying and no harassment
No leaking
No breach of collective responsibility
No misuse of taxpayer money
No actual or perceived conflicts of interest

Johnson also declared that 'The precious principles of public life enshrined in this document – integrity, objectivity, accountability, transparency, honesty and leadership in the public interest – must be honoured at all times; as must the political impartiality of our much admired civil service.'

HUNG PARLIAMENTS

The situation in which no party has a majority in the House of Commons is known as a hung parliament or a situation of no overall control. In such circumstances, the Prime Minister in situ continues in office until a majority can be created through a coalition with other parties. The alternative is to try to continue with a minority Government, perhaps bolstered by a 'confidence and supply' agreement with another party to ensure votes on key issues. If neither is possible, the Prime Minister resigns and the opportunity is passed to an Opposition party leader to try to put together a majority or to govern without a majority. The most recent hung parliaments have resulted from general elections in 1974, 2010 and 2017.

ELECTORAL FAILURES OF PRIME MINISTERS

Future Prime Ministers who failed on their first attempts to enter Parliament.

Prime Minister	Year	Constituency	Votes/Share	Pos
Winston Churchill	1899*	Oldham†	11,477/23.6%	3rd
Anthony Eden	1922	Spennymoor	7,567/27.6%	2nd
Harold Macmillan	1923	Stockton-on-Tees‡	11,661/34.3%	2nd
Alec Douglas-Home	1929	Coatbridge§	9,210/30%	2nd
Margaret Thatcher	1950	Dartford	24,490/36.2%	2nd
	1951	Dartford	27,760/40.9%	2nd
John Major	1974	St Pancras North	7,926/29.1%	2nd
	1974	St Pancras North	6,602/27.3%	2nd
Tony Blair	1982*	Beaconsfield	3,886/10.4%	3rd
Gordon Brown	1979	Edinburgh South	15,526/34.3%	2nd
David Cameron	1997	Stafford	20,292/39.2%	2nd
Theresa May	1992	Durham North West	12,747/27.6%	2nd
	1994*	Barking	1,976/10.4%	3rd
Boris Johnson	1997	Clwyd South	9,091/23.1%	2nd
Liz Truss	2001	Hemsworth	7,400/21%	2nd
	2005	Calder Valley	17,059/35.7%	2nd

* By-election.

† After becoming an MP, lost elections in Manchester North-West (1908),
Dundee (1922) and Leicester West (1923).

‡ Elected to the same seat in 1924, lost it again in 1929, reclaimed it in 1931,
lost it again in 1945.

§ Also lost in Lanark in 1945, having held the seat since 1931.

LORD PRIVY SEAL

The Great Seal of the Realm is used to authenticate parliamentary documents and confirms the approval of the Monarch. The Lord Keeper of the Great Seal is the Lord Chancellor. The Privy Seal was applied to documents that did not require the Great Seal or were on their way to obtaining the Great Seal. Its use is now obsolete but its official custodian is still known as Lord Privy Seal. The post is mostly ceremonial but it does allow the holder to become a member of the Cabinet without taking any particular brief – effectively Minister without Portfolio – although the office is often combined with that of the Leader of the House of Commons or Leader of the House of Lords.

SELECT COMMITTEES AND JOINT COMMITTEES

House of Commons Committees
Small cross-party groups of backbench MPs that are drawn together to look closely at a particular issue are known as Select Committees. Under the supervision of a chairman elected by fellow MPs, their investigations normally centre on the work of individual Government departments, with an emphasis on policies, expenditure and administration. They have the power to call in officials for questioning and also expert outside opinion, as well as to request the attendance of ministers and to demand information from the Government. The hearings of the committee are held in public and, when their deliberations are complete, a report is published on the findings, to which the Government is expected to respond, usually within 60 days. The chairmanship of Select Committees is allocated proportionately, based on the number of MPs each party

has in the House of Commons, with the largest party able to claim more than other parties, although certain Select Committees, such as the Public Accounts and the Standards Committees, are always chaired by an Opposition MP.

House of Lords Committees
In the House of Lords, Select Committees – some permanent, others temporary – look at subjects such as Science and Technology and Economic Affairs, rather than the work of Government departments.

Joint Committees
Committees that bring together MPs and Members of the House of Lords are known as Joint Committees. These operate in a similar way to Select Committees. Some are permanent, such as those on Human Rights and National Security; others are temporary, put together to address an issue of particular importance at the time.

THE FIRST PRIME MINISTERIAL DEBATE

The UK's first televised prime ministerial debate took place on 15 April 2010. The leaders of the three largest parties – Prime Minister Gordon Brown (Labour), David Cameron (Conservative) and Nick Clegg (Liberal Democrats) – met in Manchester before a public audience in an event broadcast by ITV and hosted by Alastair Stewart. The discussion ranged from spending cuts to tax and political reform, and snap opinion polls suggested that the winner of the debate was Clegg. The debate was followed by two similar events, held in Bristol and Birmingham, later in the month.

THE LARGEST AND SMALLEST MAJORITIES IN THE 2019 GENERAL ELECTION

Constituency	MP	Majority
Largest		
1 .... Knowsley	George Howarth *Lab*	39,942
2 .... Bethnal Green & Bow	Rushanara Ali *Lab*	37,524
3 .... Liverpool Riverside	Kim Johnson *Lab*	37,043
4 .... Bootle	Peter Dowd *Lab*	34,556
5 .... Hackney South & Shoreditch	Meg Hillier *Lab*	33,985
6 .... Camberwell & Peckham	Harriet Harman *Lab*	33,780
7 .... Hackney North & Stoke Newington	Diane Abbott *Lab*	33,188
8 .... East Ham	Stephen Timms *Lab*	33,176
9 .... Lewisham Deptford	Vicky Foxcroft *Lab*	32,913
10 ...... Sleaford & North Hykeham	Caroline Johnson *C*	32,565
Smallest		
641 .... Bolton North East	Mark Logan *C*	378
642 .... Dagenham & Rainham	Jon Cruddas *Lab*	293
643 .... Alyn & Deeside	Mark Tami *Lab*	213
644 .... Coventry North West	Taiwo Owatemi *Lab*	208
645 .... Caithness, Sutherland & Easter Ross	Jamie Stone *LD*	204
646 .... Kensington	Felicity Buchan *C*	150
647 .... East Dunbartonshire	Amy Callaghan *SNP*	149
648 .... Bedford	Mohammad Yasin *Lab*	145
649 .... Bury North	James Daly *C*	105
650 .... Fermanagh & South Tyrone	Michelle Gildernew *SF*	57

SPECIAL ADVISERS (SPADS)

A Special Adviser (or SPAD) is a temporary civil servant appointed to assist Government ministers by providing specialist advice on a subject or, more generally, helping with long-term planning or communications and other presentational issues, such as writing speeches or delivering information to backbenchers and the media. The role, which dates from 1964, is a political one, in contrast with the apolitical role of other civil servants. SPADs are appointed by Cabinet ministers, with the sanction of the Prime Minister, and may move from department to department with the same minister, but they are not allowed to formally represent the Government. Some ex-SPADs have become MPs themselves, including Prime Minister David Cameron.

THE LONGEST- AND SHORTEST-SERVING PRIME MINISTERS

Longest

1	Robert Walpole *W*	20 years 314 days
2	William Pitt (the Younger) *T*	18 years 343 days
3	Robert Jenkinson *T*	14 years 305 days
4	Robert Gascoyne-Cecil *C*	13 years 252 days
5	William Gladstone *Lib*	12 years 126 days
6	Frederick North *T*	12 years 58 days
7	Margaret Thatcher *C*	11 years 208 days
8	Henry Pelham *W*	10 years 191 days
9	Tony Blair *Lab*	10 years 56 days
10	Henry John Temple *Lib*	9 years 141 days

Shortest

46	Archibald Primrose *Lib*	1 year 109 days
47	Augustus Fitzroy *W*	1 year 106 days
48	William Grenville *Co*	1 year 42 days
49	Alec Douglas-Home *C*	363 days
50	John Stuart *T*	317 days
51	William Petty-Fitzmaurice *W*	266 days
52	William Cavendish *W*	225 days
53	Andrew Bonar Law *C*	211 days
54	Frederick Robinson *T*	144 days
55	George Canning *Co*	119 days

THE WESTMINSTER CHAPEL

The main chapel of the Palace of Westminster for many years was St Stephen's Chapel, constructed in the 13th century. This chapel also served as the main debating chamber of the House of Commons from 1548 but was destroyed by the fire that consumed the Palace in 1834. During the reconstruction, the floor plan of the chapel was used as the template for the current St Stephen's Hall. The Westminster chapel today is the Chapel of St Mary Undercroft, which dates from 1297 and is located in the former crypt of St Stephen's Chapel. Despite damage to the stonework, it survived the fire and has been restored as a place of worship after earlier uses as a wine cellar and a dining room for the Speaker of the House of Commons. It is also available to Members of both Houses for family weddings and christenings.

HOW VOTING TAKES PLACE

1 Votes in the House of Commons are known as 'divisions', because MPs leave the Chamber and divide into areas known as 'division lobbies' – two corridors running on either side of the Chamber, one for those voting 'aye' and one for those voting 'no'.

2 The Speaker puts a question (the term for a motion) to the House. If it is not clear from the 'ayes' or 'noes' shouted in response whether the question is supported or opposed, a division is called using the words 'Division! Clear the lobbies'.

3 Division bells are then rung all around the Parliamentary estate to summon MPs to the division lobbies, with information also displayed on electronic screens. MPs have eight minutes to arrive before the lobby doors are locked.

4 MPs physically pass through either the Aye or No lobby, with their names electronically recorded and the numbers collated by four tellers, who are MPs – two for ayes and two for noes.

5 When the lobbies are empty, the number of votes is written down. The tellers then line up by the Table of the House, with a teller from the winning side (standing closest to Opposition benches) announcing the numbers before handing the document to the Speaker for confirmation of the result and the call to 'Unlock!' (the lobby doors).

Note: Voting in the House of Lords is similar, although the move to a division there is made by the Lord Speaker, who calls 'Clear the bar!' The lobbies in the House of Lords are known as Contents and Not Contents.

LEADER OF THE OPPOSITION

Opposition in the House of Commons may be defined in two ways. The Official Opposition is a term that usually refers to just the second largest party in Parliament, as opposed to the Parliamentary Opposition, which includes all the parties not in Government. The title Leader of the Opposition was formally recognised in the 1930s and is given to the leader of the Official Opposition. Among the roles of the office is to lead MPs in the weekly Prime Minister's Questions session and to appoint the Shadow Cabinet, made up of shadow ministers who scrutinise the work of their opposite numbers in Government and formulate policies of their own that they hope to enact when ministers in Government themselves.

FREE VOTES

MPs and Members of the House of Lords normally vote along party lines, especially when 'whipped' to do so. Occasionally, however – notably when moral or ethical issues are under debate – parties do not impose a whip, leaving MPs to vote according to conscience in what is known as a free vote.

THE UK CONSTITUTION

The UK, famously, has no written constitution – no formal document that codifies the laws, rights, duties and principles on which the country should be governed. Instead, governance of the UK is based on numerous historic conventions, statutes, treaties and judicial decisions that collectively have shaped the law-making fabric of the country over centuries. Politicians are trusted to understand, respect and conform to these norms and precedents.

HEREDITARY AND LIFE PEERS

Hereditary Peers

Hereditary peers – nobles who inherit titles such as duke, earl, viscount and baron – were admitted without restriction to the House of Lords until 1999, when a new law restricted their total number to 90 (plus the Earl Marshal and the Lord Great Chamberlain). The move was a compromise between Prime Minister Tony Blair, who had wanted to abolish this right for all hereditary peers, and the House of Lords itself. Should a hereditary peer die or leave the House for another reason, a by-election is held to choose a replacement. In the case of 75 of the 90 hereditary peers, voting in this by-election is restricted to hereditary peers of the same party, plus crossbenchers (neutrals); for the remaining 15 hereditary peers, who take positions such as Deputy Speaker and carry out various official duties, voting is open to all peers in the House.

Life Peers

Life peers – nobles who do not pass on their titles to their heirs – first took their seats in the House of Lords in 1958, after the passage of the Life Peerages Act. Today, life peers are appointed by the Monarch on the recommendation of the Prime Minister, with some recommendations also allowed from other party leaders. Those honoured include former MPs and people from outside Parliament who have been successful in industry or in other walks of life.

ROTTEN BOROUGHS

The term 'rotten borough' was applied in the early 19th century to parliamentary constituencies that enjoyed representation disproportionate to the size of their populations. Generally, these were towns or areas that were once substantial but had, by this point, diminished dramatically. Some were allocated two MPs and many had fewer than 50 voters. An alternative name used for some of these constituencies was 'pocket borough' since control of the constituency was in the hands of an aristocratic family who owned the land and manipulated the electorate. Fifty-six of these rotten boroughs were abolished through the Reform Act of 1832 and absorbed into neighbouring constituencies. The following were some of the 'rottenest'.

Constituency	Voters	MPs	Constituency	Voters	MPs
Bramber	17	2	Old Sarum	<11	2
Callington	225	2	Plympton Earle	54	2
Dunwich	33	2	Steyning	118	2
East Looe	38	2	Weobley	93	2
Gatton	7	2	Yarmouth IoW	12	2

THE GUILLOTINE AND PROGRAMME ORDERS

Where a Government wishes to curtail the amount of time spent on debating a bill – perhaps to overcome delaying tactics by opponents – it can introduce what is known as a guillotine motion (or allocation of time motion) which, if passed, sets a date for a particular stage of the debate to end. The guillotine is rarely used these days as, since 1998, the Government has preferred to use so-called programme motions, which set out earlier in the process a precise timetable for the progress of a bill through the House.

A CONSTITUTIONAL MONARCHY

The United Kingdom has a constitutional monarchy, or limited monarchy, meaning that the powers of the Monarch are defined and restricted by the constitution of the country, as opposed to an absolute monarchy in which the Monarch has complete authority. In effect, this means that, while the Monarch remains the head of state and has formal and ceremonial powers, it is the Government that actually makes the rules. Other constitutional monarchies include Belgium, the Netherlands, Norway, Spain and Sweden.

SOME UK POLITICAL NICKNAMES

Nickname	Politician
Bambi	Tony Blair
Beast of Bolsover	Dennis Skinner
BoJo	Boris Johnson
Chingford Skinhead	Norman Tebbit
Coroner	Neville Chamberlain
Dishy Rishi	Rishi Sunak
Dizzy	Benjamin Disraeli
Doris Karloff	Anne Widdecombe
Eggwina	Edwina Currie
Flashman	David Cameron
Gorbals Mick	Michael Martin
Grand Old Man	William Gladstone
Iron Lady	Margaret Thatcher
Mad Monk	Keith Joseph
Maybot	Theresa May
Ming the Merciless	Menzies Campbell
Prince of Darkness	Peter Mandelson
Red Ken	Ken Livingstone
Squiffy	Herbert Asquith
Sunny Jim	James Callaghan
Supergrass	Ian Gow
Supermac	Harold Macmillan
Tarzan	Michael Heseltine
Two Brains	David Willetts
Two Jags	John Prescott
Vulcan	John Redwood
Welsh Windbag	Neil Kinnock
Welsh Wizard	David Lloyd George

THE STATE OPENING OF PARLIAMENT

The State Opening of Parliament, which takes place at the start of each new Parliamentary session or shortly after a general election, is the only regular occasion when the three constituent parts of the UK Parliament – the Crown, the House of Commons and the House of Lords – come together.

1 Parliament is officially opened by the Monarch who travels to Westminster from Buckingham Palace by horse-drawn coach as part of a showpiece procession.

2 At the Palace of Westminster, the Monarch is robed and crowned before processing through to the House of Lords (during the Covid pandemic and on a few other occasions, the ceremony has been pared back and, along with other symbols of authority, the Imperial State Crown has been carried before the Monarch, rather than worn).

3 The official known as Black Rod is dispatched from the Lords to the Commons to summon MPs to hear the Monarch's speech, which is not written by the Monarch but by the Government and outlines its new legislative programme.

4 MPs then return to the Commons to begin several days of debate on the measures announced.

GREEN PAPERS AND WHITE PAPERS

Whenever a Government wishes to invite constructive feedback on a policy proposal that is still in its formative stages, it will issue a 'green paper' – a consultation document that is accessible to MPs and other interested parties for their comments, which may or may not be taken on board. In contrast, more developed statements of policy intent are published in a 'white paper'.

A CHEQUERED HISTORY

Chequers, or Chequers Court, is the official country residence of the UK Prime Minister.

The house stands in 1,500 acres of parkland near the village of Ellesborough in Buckinghamshire and dates back to the 12th century when the owner was one Elias Ostarius, whose name may be the source of the name of the property: an ostarius was an usher in the Court of the Exchequer and this particular Ostarius apparently incorporated a chess board – traditionally used as counting table – in his coat of arms.

The current building dates from the 16th century when the sister of Lady Jane Grey, the disputed nine-day queen of 1553, was held prisoner there. The house is also linked to Oliver Cromwell, whose grandson married its owner in 1715.

The property was remodelled in the 19th century and was used as a hospital for a while during the First World War, before its last owners, Lord and Lady Lee of Fareham, donated it to the nation in 1917 for use as a rural retreat for the Prime Minister.

In the 1990s, Norma Major, the wife of Prime Minister John Major, wrote a book about the history of the building.

SEARCHING THE CELLARS

The legacy of the Gunpowder Plot lives on. In 1605, Guy Fawkes and other Catholic conspirators attempted to assassinate the Protestant King James I by blowing up the House of Lords during the State Opening of Parliament. To this day – just to be on the safe side – before every State Opening, the cellars of the Palace of Westminster are formally searched for explosives by the Yeomen of the Guard (the ceremonial bodyguards of the Monarch).

37

SOME MPS NOTED IN OTHER FIELDS
BEFORE ENTERING PARLIAMENT

MP	Profession	Years as MP
Leo Amery *C*	journalist	1911–45
Louise Bagshawe* *C*	author	2010–12
Martin Bell *Ind*	journalist/broadcaster	1997–2001
Hilaire Belloc *Lib/Ind*	poet/author	1906–10
Horatio Bottomley *Lib/Ind*	journalist	1906–12; 1918–22
Tracy Brabin *Lab*	actor	2016–21
Gyles Brandreth *C*	author/humourist	1992–97
John Buchan *C*	author	1927–35
Menzies Campbell *Lib/LD*	athlete	1987–2015
Christopher Chataway *C*	athlete/broadcaster	1959–66; 1969–74
Geoffrey Chaucer†	poet	1386
Sebastian Coe *C*	athlete	1992–97
Bill Deedes *C*	journalist	1950–74
Benjamin Disraeli *C*	author	1837–81
Andrew Faulds *Lab*	actor	1966–97
Michael Foot *Lab*	journalist	1945–55; 1960–92
Norman Fowler *C*	journalist	1974–2001
Clement Freud *Lib*	writer/gourmet	1973–87
Ian Gilmour *C*	journalist	1962–92
Michael Gove *C*	journalist	2005–
Douglas Hurd *C*	author	1970–97
Glenda Jackson *Lab*	actor	1992–2015
Boris Johnson *C*	journalist	2001–08; 2015–
Nigel Lawson *C*	journalist	1974–92
Henry Longhurst *C*	golf journalist	1943–45
Iain Macleod *C*	journalist	1950–70
Esther McVey *C*	broadcaster	2010–15; 2017–
Andrew Marvell†	poet	1659; 1660–78
Austin Mitchell *Lab*	journalist/broadcaster	1977–2015
Colin Moynihan *C*	rower	1983–92
Chris Mullin *Lab*	author	1987–2010
Isaac Newton *W*	mathematician/scientist	1689–90; 1701–02
Joseph Paxton *Lib*	gardener/architect	1854–65
Richard Brinsley Sheridan *W*	author/playwright	1780–1812
Giles Watling *C*	actor	2017–

* MP under her married name of Louise Mensch. † Pre-political party era.

THE CABINET

The senior ministers in a Government are known collectively as the Cabinet, a term derived from the small room in which the closest advisors of a Monarch traditionally would have gathered. The full name is actually Cabinet Council, which contrasts with Privy Council, as is outlined below.

THE PRIVY COUNCIL

Deriving its name from the fact that it once served as the private advisory body to the Monarch, the Privy Council is a body of distinguished parliamentarians, lawyers, clergymen and other eminent citizens, currently totalling around 650 in number.

The role of the Privy Council was diminished in the mid-17th century with the development of the Cabinet (or· Cabinet Council), a smaller body of close advisors to the Monarch (and later the Prime Minister). Today, while the Privy Council retains certain functions, relating to charters and judicial matters, its role is marginal.

A presence on the Privy Council is largely honorific: full meetings – held at St James's Palace – only take place on the accession of a new Monarch or if a Monarch intends to marry.

Membership of the Privy Council confers the right to be addressed as 'the Right Honourable'. Ministers and archbishops, along with the Leader of the Opposition, are automatically appointed, with other appointments (for life) made by the Monarch on the recommendation of the Prime Minister.

All Privy Council members take an oath of secrecy, which allows ministers to access Cabinet papers and selected Opposition party leaders to review sensitive national security information whenever this is considered to be appropriate.

THE HOSTAGE MP

In a ritual dating back to King Charles I, whose relationship with Parliament was somewhat contentious and ended with his execution in 1649, the Monarch's safe return from the State Opening of Parliament is always guaranteed by holding one MP 'hostage' at Buckingham Palace. The MP (usually a backbencher) is released once the Monarch is back in residence.

EXTENSION OF THE FRANCHISE

The right to vote in UK parliamentary elections was, for many centuries, subject to tight restrictions and corrupt practices. Reforms during the 19th century opened up the franchise to more voters, balancing out geographical inequalities and allowing more working-class men to participate, but, despite this, still only a quarter of the adult population became eligible to vote. In 1918, previous regulations were finally repealed and new franchise arrangements, based on residency rather than property ownership, came into law. Some women were given the right to vote at the same time. Significant further changes to the franchise have been enacted since.

Year	Extension To
1918	Men over 21; women over 30
1928	Women over 21
1969	Men and women over 18

MPS WHO HAVE DIRECTLY CROSSED THE FLOOR IN RECENT TIMES

Year	MP	Party Left	Party Joined
1995	Alan Howarth	Conservative	Labour
1995	Emma Nicholson	Conservative	Liberal Democrats
1997	George Gardiner	Conservative	Referendum
1999	Shaun Woodward	Conservative	Labour
2001	Paul Marsden	Labour	Liberal Democrats
2005	Robert Jackson	Conservative	Labour
2007	Quentin Davies	Conservative	Labour
2014	Douglas Carswell	Conservative	UKIP
2014	Mark Reckless	Conservative	UKIP
2019	Phillip Lee	Conservative	Liberal Democrats
2021	Kenny MacAskill	SNP	Alba
2021	Neale Hanvey	SNP	Alba
2022	Christian Wakeford	Conservative	Labour

Note: In addition, numerous MPs have left a party to become 'independent', many as a result of the whip being removed temporarily for disciplinary reasons and others because of major policy differences. Some of these independents have later become members of other parties – including, in 2019, the tranche of MPs from both the Conservative and Labour parties who later formed Change UK.

VOTING SYSTEMS IN THE UK

UK Parliament:
First Past the Post

Voters in each constituency are given a list of candidates and place a cross next to the one they wish to elect. The candidate gaining the most votes is elected.

Scottish and Welsh Parliaments:
Additional Member System

Election to the Scottish and Welsh Parliaments is through a two-tier system. The first tier, with its own ballot paper, sees one representative elected from each constituency on a first-past-the-post basis. This vote is counted first. The second tier, using a separate ballot paper, is based on regions (Scotland has eight regions, Wales has five), with several representatives (seven in Scotland, four in Wales) elected per region. For this regional ballot, parties, rather than party candidates, are listed (along with candidates with no party affiliation) and voters simply mark which one has their preference. But, rather than the party or person with the most votes simply being elected, a calculation is made to try to balance out the support each has within the region. This involves taking the total number of votes received and dividing this by 1 + the number of elected members the party has already won in the region's constituencies. The party or person with the highest resulting score is elected and then the calculation is made again but updated to include the seat that has just been allocated. The process continues until all the representatives have been elected.

Northern Ireland Assembly:
Single Transferable Vote (STV)

Instead of just one representative per constituency, there are several. Electors number a list of candidates according to their preferences – 1 for favourite, 2 for next favoured and so on. Parties often enter more than one candidate per constituency and electors may indicate as many preferences as they wish. Based on the number of representatives available and the number of votes cast, a set number of votes (the 'quota') is established for a candidate to be elected. Once a candidate has reached this threshold and is elected, any additional votes for that candidate are not counted but the second preferences on those votes are counted instead and – given a fractional value based on the number of votes the candidate has received above the threshold – are distributed among the other candidates accordingly. If no candidate passes the threshold for election, the candidate with the fewest votes is eliminated and their second preferences are distributed. The process continues until all the seats have been filled.

RECENT GENERAL ELECTION
PARTY CAMPAIGN SLOGANS

1979 ..Conservative*..*Labour Still Isn't Working*
      Labour................................ *The Labour Way Is the Better Way*
      Liberal ....*The Real Fight Is for Britain – Go Liberal*
1983 ..Conservative*................................ *The Challenge of Our Times*
      Labour................................ *The New Hope for Britain*
      SDP-Liberal Alliance................ *Working Together for Britain*
1987 ..Conservative*................................ *The Next Moves Forward*
      Labour................................ *Britain Will Win with Labour*
      SDP-Liberal Alliance.................. *Britain United – The Time Has Come*
1992 ..Conservative*................................ *The Best Future for Britain*
      Labour................................*It's Time to Get Britain Working Again*
      Liberal Democrats............................*Changing Britain for Good*
1997 ..Conservative .... *New Labour, New Danger*
      Labour*................................ *Britain Deserves Better*
      Liberal Democrats................................ *Make the Difference*
2001 ..Conservative ....*Time for Common Sense*
      Labour*................................*Schools and Hospitals First*
      Liberal Democrats................................*Freedom Justice Honesty*
2005 ..Conservative .... *Are You Thinking What We're Thinking?*
      Labour*.. *Forward, Not Back*
      Liberal Democrats................................ *The Real Alternative*
2010 ..Conservative*.. *Vote for Change*
      Labour.. *A Future Fair for All*
      Liberal Democrats................................
      Change That Works for You, Building a Fairer Britain
2015 ..Conservative*........................ *A Brighter, More Secure Future*
      Labour................................ *A Better Plan. A Better Future*
      Liberal Democrats................................
      Stronger Economy. Fairer Society. Opportunity for Everyone.
2017 ..Conservative*................................*Strong and Stable Leadership*
      Labour................................*For the Many, Not the Few*
      Liberal Democrats................................*Change Britain's Future*
2019 ..Conservative*................................ *Get Brexit Done*
      Labour................................*It's Time for Real Change*
      Liberal Democrats........................*Stop Brexit. Build a Brighter Future*

* Winner of most seats.

Note: Other slogans were used at times during each campaign.

THE EXCHEQUER

Back in the Norman days, before spreadsheets and calculators, the king's income and expenditure were calculated by an official who used a checked cloth and stones as a primitive form of abacus or counting table. It is from this checked cloth that the term Exchequer is derived. The Chancellor of the Exchequer is an office known to date from the reign of King Henry III.

PRIME MINISTER'S SPOUSES

There is no equivalent of the US title 'First Lady' in UK politics but the spouses of some Prime Ministers have become well known in recent times.

Prime Minister	Spouse	Year of Marriage
Winston Churchill	Clementine Hozier	1908
Anthony Eden	Clarissa Spencer Churchill*	1952
Harold Macmillan	Dorothy Cavendish	1920
Alec Douglas-Home	Elizabeth Alington	1936
Harold Wilson	Mary Baldwin	1940
James Callaghan	Audrey Moulton	1938
Margaret Thatcher	Denis Thatcher	1951
John Major	Norma Johnson	1970
Tony Blair	Cherie Booth	1980
Gordon Brown	Sarah Macaulay	2000
David Cameron	Samantha Sheffield	1996
Theresa May	Philip May	1980
Boris Johnson	Marina Wheeler*	1993
	Carrie Symonds†	2021
Liz Truss	Hugh O'Leary	2000

* Second wife. † Third wife.

FRONTBENCHERS AND BACKBENCHERS

Cabinet members and other ministers, as well as their opposite numbers in the Shadow Cabinet, are collectively known as frontbenchers, because of the seat they traditionally occupy in the House of Commons Chamber. All other Government and Opposition MPs, who do not hold office, are known as backbenchers, as they sit in the seats behind the front bench.

THE RIGHT TO VOTE

To cast a vote in a UK parliamentary election, a person must be:

Registered to vote in the constituency
Resident at a UK address or a UK citizen living abroad who has
registered to vote in the UK in the last 15 years
Aged 18 or older on polling day
A British or qualifying Commonwealth citizen or a citizen of the
Republic of Ireland
Not in prison (except on remand)
Not convicted of certain electoral crimes in the last five years
Not a Member of the House of Lords

FATHER OF THE HOUSE

'Father of the House' is a title bestowed upon the MP who has served the longest unbroken run in the House of Commons (although this is not necessarily the oldest MP). Where more than one MP has joined the House at the same election, it is the first to take the oath who has precedent for the title. Duties of the office are few but include presiding over the election of the Speaker, providing that the Father of the House is not also a minister. The Father of the House is also the first MP to take the oath of allegiance after the Speaker whenever a new Parliament is formed following a general election. The youngest MP, in contrast, is given the title 'Baby of the House'.

Note: In 2017, Prime Minister Theresa May graciously suggested that the title of Mother of the House should be accorded to Harriet Harman, as the longest-serving woman MP, but this remains an unofficial accolade.

LONDON MAYORAL ELECTIONS

Year	Elected Candidate		Runner-up	
2000	Ken Livingstone	*Ind*	Steven Norris	*C*
2004	Ken Livingstone	*Lab*	Steven Norris	*C*
2008	Boris Johnson	*C*	Ken Livingstone	*Lab*
2012	Boris Johnson	*C*	Ken Livingstone	*Lab*
2016	Sadiq Khan	*Lab*	Zac Goldsmith	*C*
2021	Sadiq Khan	*Lab*	Shaun Bailey	*C*

A RESIGNATION MATTER

Under a Resolution of the House dating from 2 March 1624, Members of Parliament are not allowed to resign their seat. Instead, should they wish to leave Parliament, they are obliged to apply for one of the following two 'Crown Steward and Bailiff' positions that, if held, would technically disqualify them from service. This is because, at one time, the holders would have been in the pay of the Monarch. Today, these two offices are only nominally paid and MPs receive no benefit from taking either. To accommodate instances where more than one MP decides to resign at the same time, each office is made available alternatively and the tenure is withdrawn as soon as another MP wishes to acquire it and leave Parliament.

Crown Steward and Bailiff of the three Chiltern Hundreds of Stoke, Desborough and Burnham

Crown Steward and Bailiff of the Manor of Northstead

PRIME MINISTERS WITHOUT A UNIVERSITY EDUCATION

William Cavendish	Andrew Bonar Law*
Charles Watson Wentworth	Neville Chamberlain†
Arthur Wellesley	Winston Churchill
Benjamin Disraeli	James Callaghan
David Lloyd George	John Major

* Attended lectures at Glasgow University as an extramural student.
† Attended Mason College, which later became the University of Birmingham.

RED BOXES

The red despatch box carried by ministers has become a badge of office but it also has a security role. While documents classified as 'Confidential' or lower can be carried in ordinary lockable briefcases, only official red boxes can carry documents that require a higher level of security (although less conspicuous, black versions of these 'red' boxes also exist). Also, each box locks at the bottom, to ensure that it is firmly closed before transportation. Many ministers keep their red boxes as souvenirs after leaving Government.

PRIME MINISTERS BY MONARCH

Monarch	PMs	Monarch	PMs
Elizabeth II	15	George IV	4
George III	13	George VI	4
Victoria	10	William IV	4
George II	5	Charles III	1
George V	5	Edward VIII	1
Edward VII	4	George I	1

Refers to the number of different PMs; some took office more than once.

DOWNING STREET

Number 10 Downing Street has been the official home of the UK Prime Minister since 1735.

The street was built by the diplomat George Downing in the 1680s, following designs by Sir Christopher Wren. Up to 20 terraced houses were constructed at the time, with the current number 10 then designated as number 5.

Initially, private tenants occupied the properties, with a Mr Chicken recorded as the last resident of number 10 before the building – by now expanded into a neighbouring larger house overlooking Horse Guards Parade – was given by King George II to the First Lord of the Treasury (Prime Minister) as a residence in perpetuity.

Robert Walpole was the first to move in but not all his successors have chosen to be resident here, preferring instead their own London properties.

The rambling, old building has been modernised, extended, refurbished and reinforced on numerous occasions and is today linked to two other houses which are officially homes to the Chancellor of the Exchequer (number 11) and the Government Chief Whip (number 12). Also co-joined is number 9, next to the street's security gates, which has been used for various Government functions and is the location of the £2.6 million media briefing room installed by Boris Johnson.

All the other properties in the street have been demolished, many to make room for the construction in 1868 of what is now known as the Foreign, Commonwealth & Development Office, opposite number 10.

QUALIFICATIONS TO BECOME AN MP

At least 18 years old
British citizen, a citizen of the Republic of Ireland or an eligible
Commonwealth citizen

THE LORD SPEAKER

Until 2006, the official who presided over the running of the House of Lords was the Lord Chancellor. Since then, that job has fallen to the Lord Speaker, an elected position that runs for five-year terms (with a maximum of two terms allowed).

The holder is a Member of the House of Lords and only Members of the House are eligible to vote in the election of the Lord Speaker.

The role is similar to that of the Speaker of the House of Commons, but is largely restricted to providing guidance for Members rather than controlling debate.

The Lord Speaker, who must relinquish any party affiliation upon election, has no vote or casting vote, does not call Members to speak or decide which amendments to legislation should be discussed. The Lord Speaker does not need to maintain order, as the House of Lords is a largely self-governing body, but does call for votes when required and has various ceremonial duties and responsibilities.

A group of around 20 Deputy Speakers assist the Lord Speaker and can preside over debates (while maintaining their right to contribute and vote during the process, if desired).

The Lord Speakers

2006	Baroness Hayman (Helene Hayman)
2011	Baroness D'Souza (Frances D'Souza)
2016	Lord Fowler (Norman Fowler)
2021	Lord McFall of Alcluith (John McFall)

CALLAGHAN'S FULL HOUSE

James Callaghan is the only MP to have held all three major offices of state – Chancellor of the Exchequer (1964–67), Home Secretary (1967–70) and Foreign Secretary (1974–76) – as well as becoming Prime Minister (1976–79).

WESTMINSTER HALL

The oldest building in the Palace of Westminster is Westminster Hall, which was completed in 1099 under King William II and used initially for feasts and celebrations.

From the late 12th century, for more than 600 years, as well as hosting coronation banquets and acting as a covered market for traders and merchants, the Hall became the home of the courts of law, where the legal system followed today by many countries was largely formulated.

Notable people who were tried in Westminster Hall include William Wallace, Sir Thomas More, King Charles I and Guy Fawkes, and it was in the Hall that Oliver Cromwell took the oath as Lord Protector in 1653.

In the early 19th century, the hall was partially rebuilt and restored as closely as possible to its original architectural style. It was because of this refurbishment work that the hall survived the disastrous fire of 1834 that destroyed the Houses of Commons and Lords: firefighters were able to use the workmen's scaffolding to access the flames threatening the wooden roof.

After the fire, the Hall became part of the reconstructed Palace, with a number of structural adjustments introduced by the architect Charles Barry.

During the Second World War, the Hall survived the bombing that destroyed the House of Commons Chamber.

Today, it is in Westminster Hall that deceased Monarchs and other notable public figures (such as Winston Churchill) lie in state before funerals and where important international statesmen (such as Nelson Mandela and Barack Obama) address both Houses of Parliament.

RECENT LEADERS OF THE
SCOTTISH NATIONAL PARTY (SNP)

1940	William Power	1969	William Wolfe
1942	Douglas Young	1979	Gordon Wilson
1945	Bruce Watson	1990	Alex Salmond
1947	Robert McIntyre	2000	John Swinney
1956	James Halliday	2004	Alex Salmond
1960	Arthur Donaldson	2014	Nicola Sturgeon

THE FIRST TV ELECTION

The first general election to be televised in the UK was the one held on 23 February 1950. The BBC broadcast the results in a programme hosted by Richard Dimbleby, but did not cover the electioneering beforehand. Analysts on the night included RB McCallum of Pembroke College, Oxford, the Australian journalist Chester Wilmot and a young David Butler, at the time still a research student at Nuffield College, Oxford, but later to establish himself as one of Britain's leading political scientists. Coverage also extended to the crowds watching the results on a big screen in London's Trafalgar Square. It is estimated that fewer than 350,000 viewers watched the broadcast, as television ownership at the time was very limited and only took off with the BBC's coverage of Queen Elizabeth's coronation in 1953.

THE PARTIES REPRESENTED IN PARLIAMENT

Alba · Alliance Party · Conservative Party · Co-operative Party
Democratic Unionist Party · Green Party · Labour Party
Liberal Democrats · Plaid Cymru · Scottish National Party
Sinn Féin* · Social Democratic and Labour Party

* Do not take their seats.
Note: Based on MPs elected at the 2019 general election.

INTERVENTIONS AND GIVING WAY

In the House of Commons, no MP (apart from the Speaker of the House) is allowed to interrupt an MP making a contribution to a debate unless that MP 'gives way' and allows what is known as an 'intervention'. Other MPs can stand up to attract attention and may ask the MP speaking to give way but it is entirely a matter for the person speaking whether to allow this. Also, MPs can only intervene in a speech and not in another intervention and the intervention must also be brief and relevant to the subject or it may be called out of order by the Speaker. It is also an observed courtesy that MPs wishing to intervene arrive in the House some time before doing so and remain there for some time afterwards. In some instances, interventions are not permitted. These include in ministerial statements, in the Chancellor's Budget speech and in the Budget response from the Leader of the Opposition. Traditionally, a new MP's maiden speech is also heard without intervention.

THE VAIN MAN'S LEGACY

Born in Ireland and educated at Harvard in the USA, Sir George Downing was a 17th-century British preacher, diplomat and MP who has left a mixed legacy. A ruthless and ambitious man, Downing was a controversial figure. He enacted some lasting reforms while working in the Treasury but also, on his forays abroad, provoked deadly conflict with the Dutch. Samuel Pepys, who worked for him, said he was a vain man and called him a villain, but his name has lasting international fame through the street he built – rather shoddily and on the cheap, in keeping with his nature – which has become the home of the Prime Minister and the focal point of British Government.

PRIME MINISTERS WHO DIED IN OFFICE

Prime Minister	Year of Death	Prime Minister	Year of Death
Spencer Compton	1743	Spencer Perceval*	1812
Henry Pelham	1754	George Canning	1827
Charles Watson-Wentworth	1782	Henry Temple	1865
William Pitt (the Younger)	1806		

* Assassinated.

Note: Henry Campbell-Bannerman died in 10 Downing Street in 1908, 17 days after relinquishing the role of Prime Minister to Herbert Asquith.

WESTMINSTER HALL DEBATES

Since 1999, some Parliamentary debates have been held from Tuesday to Thursday in the Grand Committee Room, close to Westminster Hall. These Westminster Hall Debates, as they are known, are not as confrontational as debates in other areas of Parliament: seating is arranged in a less adversarial, horseshoe-shaped pattern, amendments to motions are not permitted and no divisions follow, the aim being to discuss issues of importance that may not be aired in the House of Commons in a constructive, rather than partisan, manner. MPs submit subjects to be debated and these are then selected by ballot. One of the Deputy Speakers presides over the debate and ministers can be called to provide answers. These debates do not result in new laws, although the subjects, having gained attention, may be taken up by the Commons later. Other debates – to consider public petitions – may also be held on Monday afternoons, if agreed by the Petitions Committee.

TIED VOTES

In the event of a tied vote in the House of Commons, the Speaker – who normally has no vote – has the casting vote, but this should be exercised only according to how similar circumstances have been resolved in the past and on the principle that casting votes should not be used to create a majority in favour of a radical decision where a majority in the House does not actually exist. This means that the Speaker generally errs on the side of the status quo, unless further debate on the subject is possible. In the House of Lords, the Lord Speaker has no casting vote. Issues are resolved instead with reference to the Standing Orders (the established rules of the House).

THE MARRYING KIND

Prime Ministers who remained unmarried in office*
Spencer Compton · William Pitt (the Younger)
Arthur Balfour · Edward Heath

Prime Ministers who remarried while in office
Robert Walpole (widower) · Augustus Fitzroy (divorced)
Robert Banks Jenkinson (widower) · Boris Johnson (divorced)

* Numerous other Prime Minister were widowers by the time they took office.

CRACKING THE WHIPS

Whips (originally known as whipper-ins) are the political parties' enforcers in the House of Commons and the House of Lords. Appointed by party leaders, their job is to ensure that MPs are aware of important votes coming up and vote the correct way when the time comes. The circular they send out is known as *The Whip* and the most important votes are underlined three times in this publication, giving rise to the term 'three-line whip'. MPs who defy a three-line whip may face serious consequences, including expulsion from their party, although they do not lose their seat as an MP and can continue as an independent. Additionally, whips work with the Leader of the House of Commons to schedule business in the House and often act as tellers during divisions. They also organise the 'pairing' system for MPs who cannot attend the House to vote. The Government's Chief Whip also now holds the title of Parliamentary Secretary to the Treasury.

NAMING A MEMBER

In the House of Commons, MPs are not referred to by their names, only by the constituency they represent ('the Honourable/Right Honourable Member for …'), the position they hold ('the Minister'; 'the Secretary of State') or by a general title ('the Honourable/Right Honourable Member opposite'; 'my Honourable/Right Honourable friend'). Only the Speaker uses an MP's name, either to call them to speak or ask a question, or for disciplinary purposes. 'Naming' an MP for a breach of the rules of the House – such as the use of unparliamentary language – leads to a vote on the expulsion of the Member from the Chamber and suspension for five sitting days for an initial offence, with 20 days for a second offence and a potentially longer suspension – until the House decides it should end – for further offences. Parliamentary salaries are forfeited during these periods.

PRIME MINISTERS BORN OUTSIDE THE UK

Prime Minister	Year	Birthplace
William Petty-Fitzmaurice	1737	Dublin, Ireland*
Arthur Wellesley	1769	Dublin, Ireland*
Andrew Bonar Law	1858	New Brunswick, Canada*
Boris Johnson	1964	New York, USA

* Under British rule at the time.

I SPY STRANGERS

The House of Commons reserves the right to sit in private but in practice visitors are allowed to watch proceedings from what used to be known as the 'Strangers' Gallery'. At a time when privacy was more closely guarded, an MP could ask for visitors to be ejected by simply calling 'I spy strangers'. That call was still in use until 1998 and was somewhat misused by MPs looking to draw out a debate and waste time, knowing that the Speaker would be required to put the motion 'That strangers do now withdraw' and the galleries would have to be cleared. The modern replacement is a motion from an MP 'that the House sit in private'. The term 'Strangers' itself was replaced by 'Members of the Public' in 2004 and the 'Stranger's Gallery' is now known as the 'Public Gallery'. There is, however, still a Strangers' Bar in the Palace of Westminster, as well as an elegant Strangers' Dining Room.

A DROP OF WHAT YOU FANCY

The only MP who is allowed to drink alcohol in the House of Commons Chamber is the Chancellor of the Exchequer and only while presenting the Budget speech. Not all Chancellors take advantage of this privilege but notable exceptions include William Gladstone, who sustained himself with sherry and beaten egg; Benjamin Disraeli and Denis Healey, who both chose brandy and water; Geoffrey Howe, who opted for a gin and tonic; Nigel Lawson, who sipped a spritzer; and Kenneth Clarke – normally noted as a beer drinker – who on this occasion opted for a dram of Scotch whisky.

GOVERNMENT MAJORITIES
AT GENERAL ELECTIONS

Year	Party	Majority
1945	Labour	146
1950	Labour	5
1951	Conservative	17
1955	Conservative	60
1959	Conservative	100
1964	Labour	4
1966	Labour	98
1970	Conservative	30
1974	No majority party*	
1974	Labour	3†
1979	Conservative	43
1983	Conservative	144
1987	Conservative	102
1992	Conservative	21
1997	Labour	179
2001	Labour	167
2005	Labour	66
2010	No majority party	
2015	Conservative	12
2017	No majority party	
2019	Conservative	80

* February 1974. † October 1974.

OUTLAWRIES BILL

One of Parliament's arcane rituals is the reading of the Outlawries Bill at the start of each Parliament. On returning to the House of Commons from the House of Lords after the State Opening of Parliament, MPs are immediately presented with this bill which contains no legal proposals but emblematically underscores the principle that MPs – asserting their independence from the Monarch – have the right to debate other business before they consider the Monarch's Speech. The bill makes no progress and discussions soon move on to the Government's new legislative programme.

THE GANG OF FOUR

In 1981, the four prominent politicians listed below, all former Cabinet ministers disheartened by the Labour Party's continuing move to the left, broke away to form the Social Democratic Party (SDP). Initial support came from 13 other Labour MPs and one Conservative. While achieving some early success in by-elections, the party failed to break the Conservative-Labour Westminster duopoly and, in 1987, it merged with its electoral allies, the Liberals, to form what would become the Liberal Democrats. A rump SDP continued alone for a few more years but with very little impact.

Roy Jenkins · David Owen · Bill Rodgers · Shirley Williams

HOURS OF WORK

House of Commons Chamber
Monday 2.30pm–10.30pm
Tuesday–Wednesday 11.30am–7.30pm
Thursday 9.30am–5.30pm
Friday 9.30am–3pm*

House of Lords Chamber
Monday–Tuesday 2.30pm–10pm
Wednesday 3pm–10pm
Thursday 11am–7pm
Friday 10am–5pm†

Note: Business in both Houses may continue until much later each night.
* Only meets on Fridays 13 times during the year, in order to consider Private Members' Bills, but may be convened on other Fridays where necessary.
† Only sits on some Fridays.

THE USUAL CHANNELS

Efficient running of parliamentary business demands cooperation between the Government and Opposition parties (and particularly the Official Opposition). This requires the Leader of the House and the Shadow Leader of the House, along with party whips, to liaise behind the scenes and make compromises wherever necessary in a process known as 'the usual channels'.

A HISTORY OF PARTY POLITICAL BROADCASTS

Party Political Broadcasts and Party Election Broadcasts – short appeals made to voters by political parties – began on BBC Radio in 1924.

Viscount Samuel, leader of the Liberal Party in the House of Lords, fronted the first televised version in 1950, although this was just a recording of a radio broadcast made earlier that evening. Samuel was back, however, with the first true television broadcast a year later.

Until 1987, broadcasts went out simultaneously on the BBC and ITV.

With technical facilities and supervision initially provided by the BBC, these broadcasts were often rather leaden and fact-filled for many years but became glossier, slicker and more imaginative during the 1980s, when parties took control of production themselves.

The number of broadcasts allocated to each party is based on evidence of electoral support and, for Party Election Broadcasts, the number of seats the party is contesting.

Each broadcast is free of charge and helps compensate parties for the fact that, unlike in countries such as the USA, paid-for political commercials are not permitted on radio and television in the UK.

PAIRING

A longstanding convention of the House of Commons is the informal arrangement through which MPs who are unable to vote, because of official business or personal circumstances such as illness, are 'paired' with an opposing MP who then doesn't vote. Effectively, the opposing votes of the two MPs cancel each other out. Arrangements are made for pairing by the whips' offices and are generally well observed, although they may not be agreed for very important votes, for which a three-line whip is imposed.

PMS ON GUARD

Numerous Prime Ministers are honoured in the collection of statues and busts on display in the Members' Lobby – the hallway that leads to the House of Commons – but four PMs hold prime position at the main doors.

Clement Attlee · Winston Churchill · David Lloyd George · Margaret Thatcher

A SEATING PLAN

Convention, rather than rules, dictates where MPs sit in the Chamber of the House of Commons. The Government front bench traditionally takes the first row of seats to the Speaker's right (the 'Treasury Bench'), with the Opposition front bench taking the corresponding seats to the Speaker's left. However, there is nothing to stop other MPs occupying these seats. The Government Chief Whip normally chooses the seat closest to the gangway on the front bench and former Prime Ministers and other senior Members also have their own preferred seats, which are generally respected by their colleagues. Minority parties mostly take seats on the other side of the gangway from the front benches and their leaders tend to occupy the front or second row. Occasionally, Members belonging to a party that has a huge majority in the House may need to look for seats on the Opposition side.

RECENT LEADERS OF THE ULSTER UNIONIST PARTY

1940	John Miller Andrews	1995	David Trimble
1946	Basil Brooke	2005	Reg Empey
1963	Terence O'Neill	2010	Tom Elliott
1969	James Chichester-Clark	2012	Mike Nesbitt
1971	Brian Faulkner	2017	Robin Swann
1974	Harry West	2019	Steve Aiken
1979	James Molyneaux	2021	Doug Beattie

THE LAW LORDS AND THE SUPREME COURT

For centuries, the House of Lords played an important judicial role as the highest court of appeal of the country. At times, the whole of the House heard appeal cases but this was later changed so that cases were heard only by a panel of 12 of its members – all highly-qualified and experienced judges – known as the Law Lords. This function of the House was removed in 2009 with the establishment of the Supreme Court to take on these legal duties. The Law Lords of that time became the first justices of the Supreme Court and relinquished their right to sit or vote in the House of Lords until their retirement from the Court. The Supreme Court meets in the former Middlesex Guildhall, close to Parliament, and now stands completely separate from, and independent of, the UK's political bodies, with appointment to the panel of judges made through a selection commission.

EARLY DAY MOTIONS

An Early Day Motion (EDM) is a motion that is submitted for debate in the House by an MP, but without a date fixed for the debate to actually take place (i.e. in the hope that it will be heard on an 'early day' in the future). Because the motion may attract the signatures of, and possibly amendments from, a large number of fellow MPs, the EDM is a useful device for drawing attention to, and gaining publicity for, a particular issue, even though, in most cases, the proposed debate never actually takes place.

RECENT CHANCELLORS OF THE EXCHEQUER

1943	John Anderson	1974	Denis Healey
1945	Hugh Dalton	1979	Geoffrey Howe
1947	Stafford Cripps	1983	Nigel Lawson
1950	Hugh Gaitskell	1989	John Major
1951	Richard Butler	1990	Norman Lamont
1955	Harold Macmillan	1993	Kenneth Clarke
1957	Peter Thorneycroft	1997	Gordon Brown
1958	Derick Heathcoat-Amory	2007	Alistair Darling
1960	Selwyn Lloyd	2010	George Osborne
1962	Reginald Maudling	2016	Philip Hammond
1964	James Callaghan	2019	Sajid Javid
1967	Roy Jenkins	2020	Rishi Sunak
1970	Ian Macleod	2022	Nadhim Zahawi
1970	Anthony Barber	2022	Kwasi Kwarteng

HENRY VIII CLAUSES

House of Commons bills may occasionally include what are known as Henry VIII clauses, which allow ministers to amend or repeal laws without the full scrutiny of the House of Commons. These clauses date from a law of 1539 that allowed King Henry VIII to bypass Parliament and rule by proclamation although their use today is much more controversial. Where changing circumstances require sensible, practical adjustments to a law, MPs and Lords may be relaxed about their usage, but there is more concern when it is deemed that a Government is using these clauses to simply consolidate more power into its own hands or even to push through changes that might otherwise face stiff opposition in the House.

COINING BREXIT

The creation of the term 'Brexit', widely used to describe the process of the UK leaving the European Union, is credited to Peter Wilding, the founder and director of British Influence, a think tank that campaigned for the UK to remain in the EU. He first used the word in a blog post on 15 May 2012.

THE CABINET SECRETARY

The job of the Cabinet Secretary is to advise the Prime Minister on the workings of Government and the running of Cabinet. While the holder is the head of the Civil Service and not a politician, the role is highly influential as the task involves making sure that the Prime Minister's strategies and policies are prioritised and efficiently put into effect. The position was created in 1916 to ensure that a full account of Cabinet discussions was recorded – previously, the only record was a summary letter written by the Prime Minister to the Monarch – and, to this day, the Cabinet Secretary sits alongside the Prime Minister during Cabinet meetings to note what is debated and decided. Here is a list of the Cabinet Secretaries to date.

1916	Maurice Hankey	1998	Richard Wilson
1938	Edward Bridges	2002	Andrew Turnbull
1947	Norman Brook	2005	Gus O'Donnell
1963	Burke Trend	2012	Jeremy Heywood
1973	John Hunt	2018	Mark Sedwill
1979	Robert Armstrong	2020	Simon Case
1988	Robin Butler		

PARDON MY FRENCH

English is not the only language allowed in Parliament. Welsh is permitted in committees, with a translator on hand for non-speakers, although it is not allowed in debates in the House of Commons. Another permitted language is Norman French, which is used for some of the formal dialogue between the House of Commons and the House of Lords when a bill is passing through Parliament – a remnant of archaic procedures that have not been updated for centuries. It is also used when the Monarch gives the Royal Assent to a bill, with the Clerk of the Parliaments declaring in the House of Lords 'La Reyne/Le Roi le veult' ('The Queen/The King wishes it').

HANSARD

Hansard is the official daily record of debates, statements and other business that takes place in Parliament. *Hansard* reporters record all the business of both Houses, as well as debates in Westminster Hall and proceedings in Select Committees. After editing out repetitions and verbal mis-steps, correcting grammar, piecing together scraps of dialogue and ensuring fluency – but without altering the meaning of what was said – *Hansard* publishes the details online within a few hours and in printed form by early the following day. Bound copies of these reports, corrected for any inaccuracies, are then produced for posterity. The origins of *Hansard* lie with the Hansard family who, as printers, worked closely with Parliament from the 18th century, and in particular with Thomas Curson Hansard who began publishing reports of Parliamentary activity in the early 19th century.

RECENT LEADERS OF THE LIBERAL PARTY AND LIBERAL DEMOCRATS

Liberal Party

1945	Clement Davies	1967	Jeremy Thorpe
1956	Jo Grimond	1976	David Steel

Liberal Democrats

1988	Paddy Ashdown	2015	Tim Farron
1999	Charles Kennedy	2017	Vince Cable
2006	Menzies Campbell	2019	Jo Swinson
2007	Nick Clegg	2020	Ed Davey

Note: The Liberal Party referred to above merged with the SDP in 1988 to form the Liberal Democrats but a separate Liberal Party still exists.

GRAND COMMITTEES

A Grand Committee of the House of Commons is an assembly of all the MPs representing constituencies in Scotland, Wales and Northern Ireland, for the purpose of discussing issues of particular relevance to their nations. However, since devolution, such meetings have become rare. In the House of Lords, the term Grand Committee simply refers to an alternative debating forum that may run in parallel with activities of the House itself.

LORDS SPIRITUAL AND TEMPORAL

Members of the House of Lords are classified into two groups: Lords Spiritual and Lords Temporal. The Lords Spiritual are those from an ecclesiastical background, namely the Archbishops of Canterbury and York, and other bishops. The Lords Temporal are the life peers and the elected hereditary peers, as well as the Earl Marshal and Lord Great Chamberlain.

EARL MARSHAL AND LORD GREAT CHAMBERLAIN

The Earl Marshal is an officer of the House of Lords who has an important role in organising coronations, royal funerals, royal processions and other ceremonies, and also presides over the College of Arms (new applicants for a grant of arms require his approval). The role is hereditary and resides with the Duke of Norfolk. The Lord Great Chamberlain is another officer of the House of Lords, this time responsible for royal affairs in Parliament, including attending the Monarch at a coronation, making arrangements for the Monarch's Speech and looking after the Monarch's Robing Room and the Royal Gallery. The position is hereditary and shared by a number families who take on the official duties in turn, changing over at the start of each new royal reign, with one member of the family assuming the title.

LEADERS OF THE SOCIAL DEMOCRATIC PARTY (SDP)

1981	Roy Jenkins	1987	Robert Maclennan
1983	David Owen	1988	David Owen

Note: The SDP referred to above merged with the Liberal Party in 1988 to form the Liberal Democrats but a separate SDP still exists.

NO CONFIDENCE

When a Government is in difficulty, a vote of no confidence – also known as a censure motion – may be tabled in the House of Commons, using the wording 'That this House has no confidence in HM Government'. Should the motion succeed, a new Government that can survive a vote of confidence in the House must be formed within 14 days. Otherwise, Parliament is dissolved and a general election is called to resolve the political impasse.

LEADERS OF THE HOUSE

The Leader of the House of Commons is a Government MP (usually a Cabinet minister) with the responsibility for scheduling the Government's legislative programme, setting out which debates and other business will take place at the start of each week and accommodating backbencher interests. The Leader of the House of Lords is also a Cabinet minister appointed by the Prime Minister but has a slightly different role: as well as managing the Government's programme, they also advise the House on points of order and procedure because the Lord Speaker of the House of Lords has no mandate to rule on procedural matters. They may also be called on to represent and speak for the whole House on formal occasions.

THE NUMBER OF MPS

How the total number of Members of Parliament has changed over the years.

1945	640	1992	651
1950	625	1997	659
1955	630	2005	646*
1974	635	2010	650
1983	650		

* The introduction of the Scottish Parliament led to a reduction in the number of Scottish MPs at Westminster.

LOBBYING

At Westminster, a lobby is a meeting room or waiting area. The division lobbies are effectively waiting areas which MPs pass through in order to vote in a debate, while the Central Lobby – an octagonal area which sits at the heart of the Palace of Westminster, between the Houses of Commons and Lords – is traditionally the place where constituents, the media and other people can meet and interview MPs and peers (no appointments necessary, although advisable). From this name comes the verb to lobby, meaning to pressure MPs and, especially Government ministers, into supporting a particular cause and to make or change legislation accordingly. Lobbying is carried out by individuals, businesses, trade unions, charities and other groups, with professional lobbying firms now heavily involved.

IMPEACHMENT

Although most commonly associated with the prosecution of a President in the USA, impeachment is also a procedure available in the UK to bring to justice individuals – particularly holders of high office – who are accused of treason or other high crimes and misdemeanours that no other authority will prosecute. The concept dates back to the 14th century, to the days when the courts had very little oversight of Governmental power, and involves the Lords passing verdict on a case brought forward by the House of Commons. However, the last recorded impeachment took place in 1806, when Henry Dundas, the 1st Viscount Melville, was acquitted following charges of the misuse of public money while treasurer of the Admiralty. The procedure has now been rendered obsolete by other legal mechanisms.

WOMEN MPS

The number of women elected as Members of Parliament in general elections rose slowly throughout the 20th century but has increased notably since 1997. The figure shown for 2019 amounts to 33.8 per cent of all MPs.

1918	1	1987	41
1929	14	1997	120
1945	24	2010	143
1964	29	2019	220
1979	19		

SECONDARY LEGISLATION AND STATUTORY INSTRUMENTS

Primary legislation is the term used for the main laws passed in the House of Commons. Secondary, or 'delegated', legislation refers to laws created by the Government without the need to consult the House in detail. The most common form of secondary legislation is the statutory instrument. This allows ministers to adjust primary legislation to bring it up to date, for instance, or to incorporate measures that were not needed at the time the law was passed, so that the law remains both workable and enforceable, without the need to pass another act through Parliament. However, there are sometimes concerns that the statutory instrument has been used to avoid unwanted scrutiny of a law change or for some other nefarious reason.

RECENT FOREIGN SECRETARIES

1938	Edward Wood*	1979	Peter Carington‡
1940	Anthony Eden	1982	Francis Pym
1945	Ernest Bevin	1983	Geoffrey Howe
1951	Herbert Morrison	1989	John Major
1951	Anthony Eden	1989	Douglas Hurd
1955	Harold Macmillan	1995	Malcolm Rifkind
1955	Selwyn Lloyd	1997	Robin Cook
1960	Alec Douglas-Home†	2001	Jack Straw
1963	Richard Butler	2006	Margaret Beckett
1964	Patrick Gordon Walker	2007	David Miliband
1965	Michael Stewart	2010	William Hague
1966	George Brown	2014	Philip Hammond
1968	Michael Stewart	2016	Boris Johnson
1970	Alec Douglas-Home	2018	Jeremy Hunt
1974	James Callaghan	2019	Dominic Raab
1976	Anthony Crosland	2021	Liz Truss
1977	David Owen	2022	James Cleverly

* Viscount Halifax. † Earl of Home. ‡ Baron Carrington.

WHERE HAVE ALL THE MPS GONE?

The official term for the closure of Parliament before a general election is dissolution, which is enforced 25 working days before the voting takes place. At this point, every seat in the House of Commons becomes vacant. MPs revert to ordinary citizens until the election is held and can no longer describe themselves as Members of Parliament. Following dissolution, the Government still continues to function because ministers, despite no longer being MPs, retain ministerial titles and are allowed to continue their work.

RECENT LEADERS OF THE GREEN PARTY
(OF ENGLAND AND WALES)

2008	Caroline Lucas	2018	Jonathan Bartley, Siân Berry (shared)
2012	Natalie Bennett		
2016	Jonathan Bartley, Caroline Lucas (shared)	2021	Carla Denyer, Adrian Ramsay (shared)

TITLE ON THE 10 DOWNING STREET LETTERBOX

'First Lord of the Treasury'

NOTABLE PARLIAMENTARY BY-ELECTIONS

Year	Constituency	Significance	Winning Candidate
1945	Motherwell	SNP first seat	Robert McIntyre *SNP*
1962	Orpington	Liberal Party revival	Eric Lubbock *Lib*
1966	Carmarthen	Plaid Cymru first seat	Gwynfor Evans *PC*
1967	Hamilton	SNP breakthrough	Winnie Ewing *SNP*
1973	Lincoln	EEC entry dispute	Dick Taverne *DL**
1981	Crosby	SDP first seat	Shirley Williams *SDP*
1983	Bermondsey	Homophobia claims	Simon Hughes *Lib*
1993	Newbury	Conservative collapse	David Rendel *LD*
	Christchurch	Conservative collapse	Diana Maddock *LD*
2008	Crewe & Nantwich	Conservative revival	Edward Timpson *C*
2014	Clacton	UKIP first seat	Douglas Carswell *UK*
2016	Richmond Park	Brexit issues	Sarah Olney *LD*
2021	North Shropshire	Owen Patterson affair	Helen Morgan *LD*
2022	Wakefield	'Red Wall' revival	Simon Lightwood *Lab*
	Tiverton & Honiton	Conservative collapse	Richard Foorde *LD*

* Democratic Labour.

ABSTENTION

MPs have no formal way of registering their abstention on a vote and no official record of abstentions is kept. However, the desired effect is achieved if they remain in the Chamber during a division or walk through both the Aye and No lobbies, so that their votes are duly recorded but do not count.

DEVOLVED SPEAKERS

Each of the three devolved parliaments has its own equivalent of a 'Speaker'.

Senedd (Wales)	Scotland	Northern Ireland
Llywydd (Presiding Officer)	Presiding Officer (PO)	Speaker

CURBING THE POWER OF THE LORDS

The Parliament Acts

The balance of power between the House of Commons and the House of Lords is regulated by two Parliament Acts, passed in 1911 and 1949. These acts removed the veto of the House of Lords in relation to Commons bills and ensure that, while the House of Lords has powers to amend legislation and send it back to the House of Commons, and can potentially delay a bill for up to a year, ultimately the will of the Commons will prevail. The Acts are rarely used but provide a way of breaking any stalemate between the two Houses. Bills certified by the Speaker as 'money bills' – i.e. those dealing with taxation and other financial issues – are even more strongly protected, with the Lords prevented by the Parliament Acts from delaying these by more than a month.

The Salisbury Doctrine

A further safeguard for the Commons comes from the Salisbury Doctrine or Salisbury Convention, a tradition that the House of Lords does not vote down any proposed legislation that has been promised in a Government's pre-election manifesto. The name is derived from the 5th Marquess of Salisbury who was Leader of the Opposition in the House of Lords during the Labour Government of 1945–51 when this agreement between the Commons and the Lords was reached.

RECENT LEADERS OF PLAID CYMRU

1945 .... Gwynfor Evans	2003 .... Ieuan Wyn Jones, Dafydd Iwan, Elfyn Llwyd (shared)
1981 .... Dafydd Wigley	2006 .... Ieuan Wyn Jones
1984 .... Dafydd Ellis-Thomas	2012 .... Leanne Wood
1991 .... Dafydd Wigley	2018 .... Adam Price
2000 .... Ieuan Wyn Jones	

HOW TO LOSE YOUR DEPOSIT

To stand in a Parliamentary election, a candidate must deposit a sum of money – £150 when introduced in 1918 to deter 'frivolous' candidates, but £500 since 1985 – with the (Acting) Returning Officer in the constituency before 4pm on the nominations deadline day. This deposit is forfeited if the candidate secures less than 5 per cent (initially 12.5 per cent) of all votes cast.

ERSKINE MAY

Although the UK does not have a written constitution, it does have what amounts to a handbook on how Parliament should function. First published in 1844, *A Treatise upon the Law, Privileges, Proceedings and Usage of Parliament*, written by Thomas Erskine May, who at the time was an assistant in the House of Commons library, is the go-to work whenever Parliamentary procedure comes under question. Now in its 25th print edition, the work is also known by the shorter title of *Parliamentary Practice* but is most familiar to the Speaker and its other users simply as *Erskine May*.

STATE FUNERALS

A state funeral, organised and overseen by the Earl Marshal and approved by Parliament, is a major honour afforded normally only to Monarchs. Other citizens have received this accolade, but only four Prime Ministers are included in their number:

Arthur Wellesley · Henry John Temple
William Gladstone · Winston Churchill

A ceremonial funeral, which is organised by the Lord Chamberlain, with the approval of the Monarch but without the need for approval from Parliament, has many of the same trappings. Two Prime Ministers have been given this honour:

William Pitt (the Younger) · Margaret Thatcher

WHAT'S IN THE BOX?

When ministers and shadow ministers speak in the House of Commons, they stand at the Commons Table behind what is known as a despatch box, on top of which they often rest their notes and files. While these wooden boxes were once used to bring despatches and other documents into the House, today there are no despatches inside, only the sacred texts that MPs use when taking the oath of allegiance. The current despatch boxes were designed by the architect Sir Giles Gilbert Scott to replace those destroyed in Second World War bombing and were presented to Parliament as a gift by New Zealand, where the puriri tree, from which they are made, is native.

BOWING TO THE HOUSE

When MPs leave the Chamber of the House of Commons, they bow. This is seen as deference to the Speaker or to the rules of the House but it may simply be a throwback to the days when the Commons met in St Stephen's Chapel and MPs bowed reverentially to the altar when entering or leaving.

WHO GOES HOME?

At the end of House of Commons business each day the call of 'Who goes home?' is made by two doorkeepers. This tradition is a throwback to the days when safety in numbers helped MPs to negotiate the streets and fields of London after dark and to save money by sharing boats on the Thames.

RECENT FATHERS OF THE HOUSE

MP	Year Elected
1965 ..Robin Turton C	1929
1974 ..George Strauss Lab	1934*
1979 ..John Parker Lab	1935
1983 ..James Callaghan Lab	1945
1987 ..Bernard Braine C	1950
1992 ..Edward Heath C	1950
2001 ..Tam Dalyell Lab	1962
2005 ..Alan Williams Lab	1964
2010 ..Peter Tapsell C	1966†
2015 ..Gerald Kaufman Lab	1970
2017 ..Kenneth Clarke C	1970
2019 ..Peter Bottomley C	1975

* Previously elected in 1929 but subsequently lost seat.
† Previously elected in 1959 but subsequently lost seat.

A PINCH OF SNUFF

Smoking was banned in the Chamber of the House of Commons in 1693 but, since the 18th century, snuff has been in ready supply, with a box kept and paid for by the doorkeeper to the Chamber for the free use of all MPs.

PROROGATION

Prorogation is the term used for the formal ending of a parliamentary session – the moment when all business is terminated and progress on most bills is brought to a close. Parliament then re-opens with a Monarch's Speech and work begins on the new programme of legislation that it outlines. Between these times, Parliament is 'prorogued'. Where a general election is imminent, progrogation may take place a few days before Parliament is dissolved to allow parties to focus on their election campaigns.

PARLIAMENTARY FIRSTS FOR WOMEN

Year	First	Person
1918	MP (elected)	Constance Markievicz *SF*
1919	MP (to take her seat)	Nancy Astor *C*
1924	Minister	Margaret Bondfield *Lab*
1929	Cabinet Minister	Margaret Bondfield *Lab*
1975	Leader of the Opposition	Margaret Thatcher *C*
1979	Prime Minister	Margaret Thatcher *C*
1992	Speaker of the House of Commons	Betty Boothroyd *Lab*
1997	Leader of the House of Commons	Ann Taylor *Lab*
1998	Government Chief Whip	Ann Taylor *Lab*
2006	Foreign Secretary	Margaret Beckett *Lab*
2006	Lord Speaker	Baroness Hayman *Lab*
2007	Attorney General	Baroness Scotland *Lab*
2007	Home Secretary	Jacqui Smith *Lab*
2016	Lord Chancellor	Liz Truss *C*
2019	Defence Secretary	Penny Mordaunt *C*

THE 1922 COMMITTEE

The 1922 Committee is a committee consisting of all Conservative backbench MPs. It was founded in 1923, with its membership initially restricted to MPs elected the previous year – hence the name. Familiarly known as 'The 22', the committee meets once a week and wields considerable influence within the Conservative parliamentary party, with its chairman – a senior MP – responsible for overseeing confidence votes in the leadership and elections for a new party leader. Frontbench party members are not permitted to attend meetings, except when in opposition.

Politics in the UK

RECENT BABIES OF THE HOUSE*

MP	*Age When Elected*
1979 ..David Alton *Lib/LD*	28 years 0 months
Stephen Dorrell *C*	27 years 1 month
1981 ..Bobby Sands *AHB†*	27 years 1 month
Stephen Dorrell *C‡*	29 years 1 month
Owen Carron *AHB†*	28 years 6 months
1983 ..Charles Kennedy *SDP/LD*	23 years 6 months
1987 ..Matthew Taylor *Lib/LD*	24 years 2 months
1997 ..Chris Leslie *Lab*	24 years 10 months
2000 ..David Lammy *Lab*	27 years 11 months
2003 ..Sarah Teather *LD*	29 years 3 months
2005 ..Jo Swinson *LD*	25 years 3 months
2009 ..Chloe Smith *C*	27 years 2 months
2010 ..Pamela Nash *Lab*	25 years 10 months
2015 ..Mhairi Black *SNP*	20 years 8 months
2019 ..Nadia Whittome *Lab*	23 years 3 months

* Youngest MP.
† Anti H Block; won by-elections but did not take their seats.
‡ Regained the title following the death of Bobby Sands.

CHAIRMAN OF WAYS AND MEANS

During the Chancellor's Budget speech, the Speaker usually vacates the Chair to allow proceedings to be supervised by the principal Deputy Speaker, who is also known as the Chairman of Ways and Means. The title is a reference to the Ways and Means committee of the House that was operational from 1641 to 1967 and generated proposals for raising taxation.

THE SPEAKER'S HOUSE

Part of the trappings of office of the Speaker of the House of Commons is the tenure of The Speaker's House, a grand townhouse that occupies part of the riverside section of the Palace of Westminster, close to Westminster Bridge. Most of the complex is comprised of lavishly-appointed state rooms that are used for official business, but the Speaker also has a study where daily business is conducted and a private apartment up on the second floor.

69

RECENT HOME SECRETARIES

1940	Herbert Morrison	1985	Douglas Hurd
1945	Donald Somervell	1989	David Waddington
1945	James Chuter Ede	1990	Kenneth Baker
1951	David Maxwell Fyfe	1992	Kenneth Clarke
1954	Gwilym Lloyd George	1993	Michael Howard
1957	Richard Butler	1997	Jack Straw
1962	Henry Brooke	2001	David Blunkett
1964	Frank Soskice	2004	Charles Clarke
1965	Roy Jenkins	2006	John Reid
1967	James Callaghan	2007	Jacqui Smith
1970	Reginald Maudling	2009	Alan Johnson
1972	Robert Carr	2010	Theresa May
1974	Roy Jenkins	2016	Amber Rudd
1976	Merlyn Rees	2018	Sajid Javid
1979	William Whitelaw	2019	Priti Patel
1983	Leon Brittan	2022	Suella Braverman

WHO CANNOT BECOME AN MP

Civil servant
Police officer
Member of the armed forces
Judge
Member of the House of Lords
Bishop
Member of another country's legislature outside the Commonwealth
Prisoner serving a sentence of more than a year

Note: This is not a comprehensive list. There are many other reasons why
candidates may be disqualified.

RECENT LEADERS OF SINN FÉIN

1937	Margaret Buckley	1962	Tomás Mac Giolla
1950	Paddy McLogan	1970	Ruairí Ó Brádaigh
1952	Tomás Ó Dubhghaill	1983	Gerry Adams
1954	Paddy McLogan	2018	Mary Lou McDonald

THE WOOLSACK

The seat of the Lord Speaker (and previously the Lord Chancellor) in the House of Lords is the Woolsack, a rectangular red cushion stuffed with wool. It is thought that the seat was introduced in the reign of King Edward III as a reminder of the importance of the wool trade to the English economy.

CABAL

The term cabal is sometimes used to describe a clique of politicians, especially those engaged in secret meetings with murky intentions. The name is derived from the French word 'cabale', which itself originated in medieval Latin, but a popular spin on the source of the term is that it comes from the small group of ministers that surrounded King Charles II and was a forerunner to the modern-day Cabinet. It is said that the initials of five of this group – Clifford, Arlington, Buckingham, Ashley (Cooper) and Lauderdale – were developed into the acronym CABAL, but this seems to be purely a humorous observation rather than the true origin of the name.

FIRST MINISTERS OF SCOTLAND, WALES AND NORTHERN IRELAND

Scotland

1999 .... Donald Dewar *Lab*
2000 .... Henry McLeish *Lab*
2001 .... Jack McConnell *Lab*
2007 .... Alex Salmond *SNP*
2014 .... Nicola Sturgeon *SNP*

Wales*

1999 .... Alun Michael *Lab*
2000 .... Rhodri Morgan *Lab*
2009 .... Carwyn Jones *Lab*
2018 .... Mark Drakeford *Lab*

Northern Ireland

1998 .... David Trimble *UU*
2001 .... Reg Empey *UU†*
David Trimble *UU*
2002 .... Assembly suspended
2007 .... Ian Paisley *DUP*
2008 .... Peter Robinson *DUP*
2010 .... Arlene Foster *DUP†*
Peter Robinson *DUP*
2015 .... Arlene Foster *DUP†*
2016 .... Arlene Foster *DUP*
2017 .... Assembly suspended
2020 .... Arlene Foster *DUP*
2021 .... Paul Givan *DUP*
2022 .... Assembly suspended

* Initially the position was known as First Secretary. † Acting First Minister.

THE PAYROLL VOTE

The Payroll Vote is an informal term used to collectively describe Government ministers and parliamentary private secretaries, even though some of these positions are not, in fact, paid. MPs who are in the Payroll Vote are forbidden by the Ministerial Code from voting against the Government, or even expressing criticism of the Government, which ensures the Government of a bedrock of support (roughly one-fifth of the entire House of Commons), even when many MPs of its own party oppose a certain policy. To rebel, therefore, Payroll MPs must resign their positions.

ELECTION BYNAMES

Year	Name	Reason
1900	Khaki Election	Influenced by the continuing Boer War; term also used for later elections close to wartime
1918	Coupon Election	'Coupon' letter issued in support of Liberals and Conservatives who favoured a continued coalition
1929	Flapper Election	Women aged 21–29 given vote for the first time

PROXY VOTING

MPs taking leave after the birth or adoption of a new child, a miscarriage or infant care issues are able to vote in the House of Commons by proxy, with another MP voting on their behalf. The first person to benefit from this system was the Labour MP Tulip Siddiq in 2019. Proxy voting was also allowed for medical and public health reasons during the Covid pandemic.

THE GREEN AND THE RED

Furnishings, fabrics, stationary and other items in the Houses of Parliament are colour coded, as is most obviously evident in the colours of the benches in the two Chambers. In the House of Commons, the colour is green, while in the House of Lords the colour is red. These colours have been used for centuries but their origin is not certain, with perhaps the Lords being red as this is traditionally a royal colour and Commons being green because of the colour's connections to nature, because it was a colour favoured by certain Monarchs or even because green materials at one time were cheaper.

HUMBLE ADDRESS

A Humble Address is a communication sent to the Monarch from one of the Houses of Parliament. Occasionally, the Opposition may use this as a device on Opposition Days to acquire papers and documents from a reluctant Government. Unlike other Opposition Day motions, if this is agreed, it is believed to be binding, meaning the Government has to comply.

BANDITS AND HORSE THIEVES

The widely-used nickname of the Conservative Party – the 'Tories' – actually dates back to 17th-century Ireland when Tories were impoverished outlaws and bandits who preyed on English settlers. Later, the term was applied to those who opposed plans to ban the Catholic James, Duke of York (later King James II), from taking the throne. This faction evolved into the Tory Party, which then changed its name to the Conservative Party when it began to adopt electoral and social reform measures around 1830. The Tories' great rivals in the debate over King James II and other matters were the Whigs, whose name also had origins in banditry, in this case referencing Scottish horse thieves. In the mid 19th century, leading Whig politicians were instrumental in establishing the Liberal Party, when they joined rebel Conservatives and other radical thinkers to oppose the governing Tories.

LEADERS OF THE
SOCIAL DEMOCRATIC AND LABOUR PARTY (SDLP)

1970	Gerry Fitt	2010	Margaret Ritchie
1979	John Hume	2011	Alasdair McDonnell
2001	Mark Durkan	2015	Colum Eastwood

Note: Party founded in 1970.

ORDER PAPERS

The business to be conducted each day in the House of Commons – both in the Chamber and in committee – is published in what is known as an Order Paper. MPs are known to wave this frantically, in place of clapping, whenever their side of the House achieves a significant victory in a vote.

THE LORD CHANCELLOR

The Lord Chancellor, or Lord High Chancellor, is appointed by the Monarch on the advice of the Prime Minister. It is a position that dates back to the 11th century but the role has changed considerably in recent years.

Until reforms to the Constitution in 2005, the Lord Chancellor acted as the Speaker of the House of Lords, but then the role was given to the holder of the new position of Lord Speaker. At the same time, the Lord Chancellor ceased to be the head of the judiciary in England and Wales, with that role given to the Lord Chief Justice.

Instead, the Lord Chancellor has become the Secretary of State for Justice, who is a member of the Cabinet and oversees, rather than manages, the judiciary. Because the Lord Chancellor no longer sits as a judge on important cases, it is now not considered essential that the holder of the office has a legal background.

One retained role is as Lord Keeper of the Great Seal – the custodian of the Great Seal of the Realm, which is used on important documents to indicate the Monarch's assent.

The Lord Chancellor is also the person who presents the Monarch with the speech during the State Opening of Parliament.

In 2016, the Conservative MP, and future Prime Minister, Liz Truss became the first woman to be sworn in as Lord Chancellor, although some historians claim that the role had been held by another woman, Eleanor of Provence, the wife of King Henry III, during the 13th century.

OPPOSITION DAYS

While most of the business of Parliament is dictated by the Government, 20 days per session are allocated to the Opposition for consideration of any business it wants to bring forward. Of the 20 days, 17 are allocated to the Official Opposition and three to the second largest Opposition party, which may be shared with other smaller parties. Additional Opposition Days are occasionally allocated if, for example, the Parliamentary session is particularly long. Votes taken on motions put forward on Opposition Days are seen as non-binding: they do not have to be taken forward into law. However, it can prove embarrassing for the Government if the motions are critical of Government policy and attract the support of a majority of MPs.

MOVING THE WRIT

Parliamentary by-elections may result if an MP dies, resigns or is deemed ineligible to continue in the role for some reason. The process of calling a by-election normally begins with the Chief Whip of the party whose MP last held the vacant seat 'moving the writ' in the House of Commons. This is basically a request for the Speaker to instruct officials to issue a writ for the election of a new MP. The Speaker puts the question to the House and, on agreement, makes the arrangements. The by-election is normally held within three months of the writ being moved, with a neighbouring MP of the same party usually taking care of the constituents' interests in the interim.

THE LARGEST AND SMALLEST CONSTITUENCIES

Constituency	Size	MP
By Area		
Largest ....Ross, Skye and Lochaber............... 12,000 km²		*SNP*
Smallest ....Islington North .... 7.35 km²		*Lab*
By Electorate		
Largest ....Isle of Wight................................. 113,021		*C*
Smallest ....Na h-Eileanan an Iar...................... 21,106		*SNP*

Note: Figures relate to the 2019 general election.

A THING ABOUT HATS

Hats have long held a strange significance in the Westminster Parliament. For centuries, they were used by MPs to reserve places in the House of Commons although men MPs wearing a hat were not (and still are not) allowed to speak in the Chamber (the rule does not apply to women MPs). Conversely, until 1998, the wearing of a hat was actually a requirement for an MP wishing to make a point of order during a division and a couple of collapsible opera hats were therefore maintained in the House to allow this Pythonesque ritual to continue. Even today, during the Speaker's procession that heralds the start of business in the House of Commons, one of the policemen on duty in the Central Lobby will shout 'Hats off, Strangers', to demand the respect of onlookers. Very few hats need to be doffed by spectators these days, but the policemen present do remove their helmets.

MOTHER OF PARLIAMENTS

The Westminster Parliament is sometimes referred to as the 'Mother of Parliaments', in recognition of the example it has set over time for other parliaments around the world. The term was coined by the Liberal politician John Bright in a speech in Birmingham in 1865, but what Bright was actually referring to was England as a country, and not Parliament itself.

QUORUM

While debates may take place in Parliament with fewer members in attendance, the minimum number of members who need to be present for a division to be valid is known as a quorum (a term literally meaning 'of whom' in Latin). In the House of Commons the quorum is 40, a figure that includes the Speaker or chair of the debate. In the House of Lords it is 30.

LEADERS OF THE
DEMOCRATIC UNIONIST PARTY*

1971 .... Ian Paisley	2021 .... Edwin Poots
2008 .... Peter Robinson	2021 .... Jeffrey Donaldson
2015 .... Arlene Foster	

* Party founded in 1971.

MAIDEN SPEECH

A maiden speech is the first speech made by a newly-elected MP in the House of Commons. The speech is usually fairly brief and, while ostensibly related to matters being debated at the time, is generally non-contentious, allowing Members on all sides of the House to hear the speech respectfully, with no interruptions. Mention is traditionally made of the MP's predecessor in the role and the character of the constituency, and the next MP to speak customarily responds with some kind remarks. There is no obligation to make a maiden speech and a new MP may instead opt to speak more directly and plainly on another matter as part of a debate, although thereafter the right to a maiden speech is forfeited. However, new MPs can still ask questions and intervene on other speeches without losing this right.

BIG BEN

An enduring symbol of the Palace of Westminster is its famous clock tower, commonly known as Big Ben, although technically Big Ben is the name of the clock's largest bell (the hour bell).

The 320-foot tower was constructed during the rebuilding of the Palace in the mid-19th century, with the clock itself built by the Dent company, according to the designs of Edmund Beckett Denison.

The original Big Ben bell was cast near Stockton-on-Tees but cracked during testing and was replaced by a bell from the Whitechapel Bell Foundry in London. Its chimes first rang out in 1859.

The clock is wound three times a week and pre-decimal pennies are used to adjust the weight of the pendulum mechanism that keeps the clock accurate to within a couple of seconds a week.

The hands of the clock roughly measure 14 feet (the long hands) and nine feet (the short hands).

The name 'Big Ben' is said to be a reference to the Welsh MP Sir Benjamin Hall, the commissioner of works for the project.

Since 1924 – with only a few interruptions – the chimes have been broadcast as a time signal by the BBC.

In 2012, the clock tower, known until this time as St Stephen's Tower, was renamed the Elizabeth Tower for the Queen's Diamond Jubilee.

CHIEF MOUSERS

The first cat to be bestowed with the title 'Chief Mouser to the Cabinet Office' was Larry, who arrived in 2011, but Downing Street has been home to many cats over the years, with the following all recent feline inhabitants.

Cat	Prime Minister
Nemo	Wilson
Wilberforce	Heath/Wilson/Callaghan/Thatcher
Humphrey	Thatcher/Major/Blair

Cat	Prime Minister
Sybil*	Brown
Larry	Cameron/May/Johnson/Truss
Freya*	Cameron
Palmerston†	Cameron/May/Johnson/Truss

* Chancellor of the Exchequer's cat. † Foreign Office cat.

POLITICS IN THE USA

THE US FEDERAL GOVERNMENT

Government in the USA is divided into three branches.

Executive Branch

Primarily, the President, an elected head of state who is Commander-in-Chief of the armed forces. The President, with the help of the Vice President, Cabinet officers and agencies such as the CIA, implements and executes laws created by Congress.

Legislative Branch

The House of Representatives and the Senate, collectively known as Congress, which make laws and pass them to the President for execution.

Judicial Branch

Primarily, the Supreme Court – the highest court in the country – a panel of judges appointed by the President and approved by the Senate. Lower, district courts and courts of appeal also make up the Judicial Branch.

THE GREAT SEAL OF THE UNITED STATES

Designed by Charles Thomson, Secretary of the Continental Congress, in 1782, working from ideas submitted by various artists, the Great Seal is the symbol of the independence and authority of the United States Government and is affixed to official and ceremonial documents. The artwork features an American eagle clutching in its claws an olive branch and a sheaf of arrows.

THE OFFICIAL RESIDENCE OF THE US PRESIDENT

The White House, 1600 Pennsylvania Avenue NW, Washington, DC 20500.

PRESIDENTS OF THE USA

1789	George Washington	F
1797	John Adams	F
1801	Thomas Jefferson	DR
1809	James Madison	DR
1817	James Monroe	DR
1825	John Quincy Adams	DR
1829	Andrew Jackson	D
1837	Martin Van Buren	D
1841	William Harrison	W
1841	John Tyler	W
1845	James Polk	D
1849	Zachary Taylor	W
1850	Millard Fillmore	W
1853	Franklin Pierce	D
1857	James Buchanan	D
1861	Abraham Lincoln	R
1865	Andrew Johnson	D
1869	Ulysses S Grant	R
1877	Rutherford Hayes	R
1881	James Garfield	R
1881	Chester Arthur	R
1885	Grover Cleveland	D
1889	Benjamin Harrison	R
1893	Grover Cleveland	D
1897	William McKinley	R
1901	Theodore Roosevelt	R
1909	William Taft	R
1913	Woodrow Wilson	D
1921	Warren Harding	R
1923	Calvin Coolidge	R
1929	Herbert Hoover	R
1933	Franklin Roosevelt	D
1945	Harry Truman	D
1953	Dwight Eisenhower	R
1961	John F Kennedy	D
1963	Lyndon Johnson	D
1969	Richard Nixon	R
1974	Gerald Ford	R
1977	Jimmy Carter	D
1981	Ronald Reagan	R
1989	George HW Bush	R
1993	Bill Clinton	D
2001	George W Bush	R
2009	Barack Obama	D
2017	Donald Trump	R
2021	Joe Biden	D

THE DECLARATION OF INDEPENDENCE

It is often assumed that the US Declaration of Independence was signed on Independence Day, 4 July 1776, but it was not until 2 August that delegates from the following 13 states added their signatures to the now-famous paper.

Connecticut · Delaware · Georgia · Maryland · Massachusetts
New Hampshire · New Jersey · New York · North Carolina · Pennsylvania
Rhode Island · South Carolina · Virginia

THE WHITE HOUSE

Designed in Palladian style by the Irish-born architect James Hoban, the White House has been the official residence of the US President since the second President, John Adams, moved in, in 1800.

The site in Washington, DC, was chosen by Adams' predecessor, George Washington, and the corner stone was laid in 1792.

During the War of 1812, the property was attacked by the British and damaged by fire, although it is a misconception that the name 'White House' was generated at this time when white paint was used to cover the scorch marks. In fact, whitewash had been used on the building before this time.

The name continued to be applied colloquially by the press throughout the 19th century, before being formally adopted by Theodore Roosevelt in 1901, who favoured it over the previous official term 'Executive Mansion'.

The building has been extended and refurbished on several occasions, including in 1902 with the construction of the West Wing as the new location of the offices of the President and staff. Here, the Oval Office was added by William Taft in 1909 before being relocated to its present position, overlooking the Rose Garden, in 1934 under Franklin Roosevelt.

An East Wing was added in 1942 and more major work was completed ten years later, under Harry Truman, when the decaying interior of the White House was completely gutted and rebuilt for safety reasons.

THE PRESIDENT ELECT

A general election to choose the President of the United States takes place every four years in early November. Once the results are certified by Congress, the winning candidate is generally known by the title 'President Elect' until the inauguration ceremony, which takes place usually on 20 January. Increasingly, however, politicians and the media use this title as soon as the result of the election is called on the night of the vote. Sitting Presidents who are re-elected simply retain the title of President until the new inauguration. The term 'Office of the President Elect', while unofficial, has also entered the language, to brand the transition team that incoming Presidents put in place to ensure a smooth handover from their predecessors.

QUALIFICATIONS FOR US OFFICE

President
Natural-born citizen of the United States
At least 35 years old
Resident of the United States for at least 14 years

Senator
United States citizen for at least nine years
At least 30 years old
Resident of the state to be represented

Representative (Congressman/woman)
United States citizen for at least seven years
At least 25 years old
Resident of the state to be represented

PRESIDENTIAL AIR TRANSPORT

Air Force One
Technically, any aircraft that has the President aboard is given the call sign 'Air Force One', although the name is now generally applied to one of two specially-adapted Boeing 747-200B aircraft introduced in 1990, during the Presidency of George HW Bush. The aircraft have the tail codes 28000 and 29000 and function as a mobile office, complete with high-tech telecom facilities, a medical unit, two kitchens and a full presidential suite. They also have an in-flight refuelling capability.

Air Force Two
'Air Force Two' is the call sign that is used for aircraft with the Vice President aboard, but is generally applied to the specially-adapted Boeing 757-200 aircraft used by the VP.

Marine One
The call sign for a helicopter on which the President is travelling is 'Marine One'. However, as with the above aircraft, the name is now used for one of a series of Sikorsky White Hawk or Sea King helicopters that the President uses for short journeys. More than one of these helicopters may take off and land simultaneously to act as a decoy for the one actually carrying the President.

Marine Two
The equivalent helicopter used by the Vice President.

FIRST DOGS

Dog(s)	President	Dog(s)	President
Skip	Theodore Roosevelt	King Timahoe	Nixon
Laddie Boy	Harding	Liberty	Ford
Rob Roy	Coolidge	Grits	Carter
King Tut	Hoover	Rex	Reagan
Fala	Franklin Roosevelt	Millie	George HW Bush
Feller	Truman	Buddy	Clinton
Heidi	Eisenhower	Barney	George W Bush
Pushinka	Kennedy	Bo/Sunny	Obama
Him/Her/Yuki	Johnson	Major/Commander	Biden

Note: 'First Dog' is not an official title.
Some Presidents also had other less famous dogs.

THE SUPREME COURT OF THE UNITED STATES

The Supreme Court is the final arbiter of justice in the USA and makes the ultimate decision on cases and disputes related to laws and the Constitution. Most of the work of the Supreme Court relates to appeals against verdicts of lower courts, although it does operate as a trial court in certain instances, such as in cases against ministers, ambassadors and consuls. Since 1869, the number of justices who serve on the Supreme Court has been set at nine. Appointments are made by the President, with the approval of the Senate, and the appointments are for life, or until the justice retires (or is impeached and expelled). The current serving members of the Court are listed below.

Justice	Appointing President	Year
Clarence Thomas	George HW Bush	1991
John G Roberts*	George W Bush	2005
Samuel A Alito Jr	George W Bush	2006
Sonia Sotomayor	Barack Obama	2009
Elena Kagan	Barack Obama	2010
Neil Gorsuch	Donald Trump	2017
Brett Kavanaugh	Donald Trump	2018
Amy Coney Barrett	Donald Trump	2020
Ketanji Brown Jackson	Joe Biden	2022

* Chief Justice; the other members of the Court are Associate Justices.

THE PRESIDENTIAL TURKEY PARDON

Each November, the President of the USA ceremonially 'pardons' a turkey that has been sent to the White House for Thanksgiving. While there is a long history of turkeys enjoying a stay of execution at the behest of Presidents – including Lincoln, Kennedy, Nixon, Carter and Reagan – the first President to formally grant this pardon was George HW Bush in 1989.

PRESIDENTS WHO DIED IN OFFICE

President	Year	Cause of Death
William Harrison	1841	Pneumonia
Zachary Taylor	1850	Cholera
Abraham Lincoln	1865	Assassinated
James Garfield	1881	Assassinated
William McKinley	1901	Assassinated
Warren Harding	1923	Heart attack or stroke
Franklin Roosevelt	1945	Brain haemorrhage
John F Kennedy	1963	Assassinated

Note: See also *Assassinated Presidents* (p. 89).

THE ONE-DAY PRESIDENT?

It is commonly believed that the US had a President who only served for one day. When President Elect Zachary Taylor refused to be sworn into office on 4 March 1849, because it was a Sunday, and because there was no Vice President sworn in either, it is assumed that executive control of the country briefly passed to the next in line, the President Pro Tempore of the Senate – the Senator who who fills in as President of the Senate in the absence of a Vice President. On this occasion, the honour fell to Senator David Atchison of Missouri. The following day, Taylor duly took the oath and Atchison has since found his niche in quiz question folklore. However, historians and constitutional experts now argue that Atchison couldn't have achieved this unique feat because his term as President Pro Tempore had, in fact, expired the day before. Therefore, the conclusion is that, for one day, the US either had no President at all or Zachary Taylor had automatically become President, oath or no oath, because the President is only required by the Constitution to take the oath before executing any presidential duties.

STATES OF BIRTH OF US PRESIDENTS

Arkansas
Bill Clinton

California
Richard Nixon

Connecticut
George W Bush

Georgia
Jimmy Carter

Hawaii
Barack Obama

Illinois
Ronald Reagan

Iowa
Herbert Hoover

Kentucky
Abraham Lincoln

Massachusetts
John Adams · John Quincy Adams
John F Kennedy · George HW Bush

Missouri
Harry Truman

Nebraska
Gerald Ford

New Hampshire
Franklin Pierce

New Jersey
Grover Cleveland

New York
Martin Van Buren · Millard Fillmore
Theodore Roosevelt
Franklin Roosevelt · Donald Trump

North Carolina
James Polk · Andrew Johnson

Ohio
Ulysses S Grant · Rutherford Hayes
James Garfield · Benjamin Harrison
William McKinley · William Taft
Warren Harding

Pennsylvania
James Buchanan · Joe Biden

South Carolina
Andrew Jackson

Texas
Dwight Eisenhower
Lyndon Johnson

Vermont
Chester Arthur · Calvin Coolidge

Virginia
George Washington
Thomas Jefferson · James Madison
James Monroe · William Harrison
John Tyler · Zachary Taylor
Woodrow Wilson

Note: The above data reveals that only eight US Presidents have been born west of the Mississippi River.

PARTY COLOURS

Red is traditionally the colour of left-wing parties in politics, and blue the colour of the right – except in the US. On the American political map, states won by Republicans are shown in red and those won by Democrats are shown in blue but this is really quite a modern development. Until 2000, the media had no fixed idea of what colours to use and alternated them between parties. Then, in the Bush v Gore election, the blues and reds settled into their current roles, although there is no obvious reason why that happened.

SECRET SERVICE CODENAMES

From the earliest days of electronic communication, the US Secret Service has used codenames to describe the Presidents they are protecting. Initially, these codenames were for safety in an age when encryption of messages was not possible, but in recent times the codenames, while still useful for brevity, have become light-hearted, chosen by the President themselves, or their team, to reflect aspects of their life, character or experience. The codenames selected for the First Lady and other members of the First Family all usually begin with the same letter as the one used by the President.

President	Codename	First Lady	Codename
Harry Truman	Supervise*	Bess Truman	Sunnyside
Dwight Eisenhower	Scorecard†	Mamie Eisenhower	Springtime
John F Kennedy	Lancer	Jacqueline Kennedy	Lace
Lyndon Johnson	Volunteer	Lady Bird Johnson	Victoria
Richard Nixon	Searchlight	Patricia Nixon	Starlight
Gerald Ford	Passkey	Betty Ford	Pinafore
Jimmy Carter	Deacon‡	Rosalynn Carter	Dancer§
Ronald Reagan	Rawhide	Nancy Reagan	Rainbow
George HW Bush	Timberwolf	Barbara Bush	Tranquility¶
Bill Clinton	Eagle	Hilary Clinton	Evergreen
George W Bush	Trailblazer#	Laura Bush	Tempo
Barack Obama	Renegade	Michelle Obama	Renaissance
Donald Trump	Mogul	Melania Trump	Muse
Joe Biden	Celtic	Jill Biden	Capri

* Also known as General. † Also known as Providence.

‡ Also known as Lock Master. § Also known as Lotus Petal.

¶ Also known as Snowbank. # Tumbler when his father was President.

85

THE HANDOVER LETTER

It has become a tradition that a departing President leaves a welcome letter for their successor, offering best wishes – even to a political opponent – and some advice based on experience. Following are extracts from these letters.

George, I treasure the memories we share and wish you all the very best. You'll be in my prayers. God bless you and Barbara.

—Ronald Reagan to George HW Bush

When I walked into this office just now I felt the same sense of wonder and respect that I felt four years ago. I know you will feel that, too. I wish you great happiness here. I never felt the loneliness some Presidents have described.

—George HW Bush to Bill Clinton

You lead a proud, decent, good people. And from this day you are President of all of us. I salute you and wish you success and much happiness.

—Bill Clinton to George W Bush

Very few have had the honour of knowing the responsibility you now feel. Very few know the excitement of the moment and the challenges you will face. There will be trying moments. The critics will rage. Your 'friends' will disappoint you. But, you will have an Almighty God to comfort you, a family who loves you, and a country that is pulling for you, including me.

—George W Bush to Barack Obama

Congratulations on a remarkable run. Millions have placed their hopes in you, and all of us, regardless of party, should hope for expanded prosperity and security during your tenure...
And finally, take time, in the rush of events and responsibilities, for friends and family. They'll get you through the inevitable rough patches.

—Barack Obama to Donald Trump

Note: The text of Donald Trump's letter to Joe Biden is yet to be released.

FIRSTS FOR WOMEN IN US POLITICS

Year	First	Person/(Place)
1869	State to grant women's suffrage*	Wyoming
1872	Presidential candidate	Victoria Woodhull
1887	Mayor	Susanna Salter (*Argonia, Kansas*)
1896	State Senator	Martha Hughes Cannon (*Utah*)
1916	Member of House of Representatives	Jeannette Rankin (*Montana*)
1922	Senator (appointed)	Rebecca Felton† (*Georgia*)
1925	State Governor	Nellie Tayloe Ross (*Wyoming*)
1932	Senator (elected)	Hattie Wyatt Caraway (*Arkansas*)
1933	Cabinet member	Frances Perkins
1981	Supreme Court Justice	Sandra Day O'Connor
1984	Vice Presidential nominee (of major party)	Geraldine Ferraro
1993	Attorney General	Janet Reno
1997	Secretary of State	Madeleine Albright
2001	National Security Advisor	Condoleezza Rice
2007	Speaker of House of Representatives	Nancy Pelosi
2016	Presidential candidate (of major party)	Hillary Clinton
2021	Vice President	Kamala Harris

* The 19th Amendment to the Constitution granting nationwide women's suffrage
was adopted in 1920.

† Appointed to replace her deceased husband and served only one day.

PARDON ME?

The Constitution declares that the President has 'Power to grant Reprieves and Pardons for Offences against the United States, except in Cases of Impeachment'. This means that the President is able to exercise 'executive clemency', which may entail a full pardon (the forgiving of crimes and the restoring of civil rights) or just commutation of a sentence (shortening or cancelling imprisonment or other sanctions). Only Federal offences may be pardoned: clemency over state crimes is not within the President's remit. Pardons may be granted at any time but an increased number tend to be issued as a Presidency draws to a close, so there is much speculation during a President's final few days about which pardons they will decide to grant. The first Presidential pardon issued was by George Washington in 1795 when he granted an amnesty (a pardon for a group) to those involved in Pennsylvania's Whiskey Rebellion (an uprising against a new whiskey tax).

WATERGATE: ANATOMY OF A SCANDAL

The political scandal that proved so huge that other scandals have been given nicknames in homage (Irangate, Partygate, etc.), Watergate is a tale of political corruption, subterfuge and cover-up at the highest level of the US Government. It was the scandal that forced the resignation of President Richard Nixon when it transpired that his close associates, seemingly with his knowledge, attempted to undermine the election campaign of Senator George McGovern, his rival in the 1972 presidential contest, through burglary, wire-tapping and other dirty tricks. Here's how events unfolded.

1 Five men are arrested for breaking into the Democratic National Committee offices in the Watergate hotel and office complex in Washington, DC.

2 Investigative work by *Washington Post* journalists Bob Woodward and Carl Bernstein gradually uncovers the whole tawdry business, aided by confessions from some of the perpetrators, an enlightening court case, a televised Congressional inquiry and some inside intelligence from a mysterious FBI officer given the codename 'Deep Throat' – many years later revealed to be the high-ranking W Mark Felt.

3 The conclusion of the scandal revolves around the release of secretly-recorded discussions in the Oval Office, which Nixon initially refuses to hand over – amid other attempts at obstruction.

4 Once these are in the hands of investigators, Nixon – who won the 1972 election with a landslide after downplaying the scandal – has no choice but to tender his resignation in order to avoid impeachment.

PARTY ANIMALS

The animals used as emblems by America's two main political parties are both rather unflattering creatures. An elephant (Republicans) may have a certain lumbering charm but can also be seen as clumsy and slow-witted. It was first associated with the Republican Party in Civil War times. A donkey (Democrats), for all the love showered on this traditionally badly-treated beast of burden, is indelibly linked to the concept of stupidity. Its links to the Democratic Party date back to President Andrew Jackson, who was labelled a 'jackass' – possibly 'A Jack-ass' – by his political opponents. Both party emblems were then popularised by the 19th-century cartoonist Thomas Nast in the satirical cartoons he drew for *Harper's Weekly* magazine.

VICE PRESIDENTS OF THE UNITED STATES

Years	Vice President
1789–97	John Adams
1797–1801	Thomas Jefferson
1801–05	Aaron Burr
1805–12	George Clinton*
1813–14	Elbridge Gerry*
1817–25	Daniel Tompkins
1825–32	John Calhoun†
1833–37	Martin Van Buren
1837–41	Richard Johnson
1841	John Tyler
1845–49	George Dallas
1849–50	Millard Fillmore
1853	William King*
1857–61	John Breckinridge
1861–65	Hannibal Hamlin
1865	Andrew Johnson
1869–73	Schuyler Colfax
1873–75	Henry Wilson*
1877–81	William Wheeler
1881	Chester Arthur
1885	Thomas Hendricks*
1889–93	Levi Morton
1893–97	Adlai Stevenson
1897–99	Garret Hobart*
1901	Theodore Roosevelt
1905–09	Charles Fairbanks
1909–12	James Sherman*
1913–21	Thomas Marshall
1921–23	Calvin Coolidge
1925–29	Charles Dawes
1929–33	Charles Curtis
1933–41	John Garner
1941–45	Henry Wallace
1945	Harry Truman
1949–53	Alben Barkley
1953–61	Richard Nixon
1961–63	Lyndon Johnson
1965–69	Hubert Humphrey
1969–73	Spiro Agnew†
1973–74	Gerald Ford
1974–77	Nelson Rockefeller
1977–81	Walter Mondale
1981–89	George Bush
1989–93	Dan Quayle
1993–2001	Al Gore
2001–09	Dick Cheney
2009–17	Joe Biden
2017–21	Mike Pence
2021–	Kamala Harris

* Died in office. † Resigned from office.

ASSASSINATED PRESIDENTS

President	Assassin	Location	Year
Abraham Lincoln	John Wilkes Booth	Washington, DC	1865
James Garfield*	Charles Guiteau	Washington, DC	1881
William McKinley†	Leon Czolgosz	Buffalo	1901
John F Kennedy	Lee Harvey Oswald	Dallas	1963

* Died 79 days later in Elberton, New Jersey. † Died eight days later.

US POLITICAL DYNASTIES

Adams

The original dynasty. John Adams was the second President of the US (having previously been the first Vice President) and his son, John Quincy Adams, was the sixth President (as well as later serving as a member of the House of Representatives). Charles Adams, son of John Quincy, was a member of the House of Representatives and Ambassador to Great Britain.

Bush

A dynasty that dates back to Prescott Bush, who served as Senator for Connecticut for nine years. Prescott's son, George HW Bush, became President, as did George's son, George W Bush. Another son of 'HW', John Ellis 'Jeb' Bush, has served as Governor of Florida and, in 2016, unsuccessfully sought the Republican nomination for the Presidency.

Clinton

After Bill's term as President, wife Hillary served as Senator for New York and Secretary of State, before nearly becoming America's first woman President in 2016, losing out instead to Donald Trump.

Harrison

William Henry Harrison served as President for only 31 days but he established a dynasty that extended more than a hundred years. His son,

John Scott Harrison, was a member of the House of Representatives and John Scott's son, Benjamin Harrison, became the 23rd President. The dynasty continued up to William Henry Harrison III, Benjamin's grandson, who served in the House of Representatives.

Kennedy

Joe Kennedy, a former US Ambassador to Great Britain, was the father of President John F Kennedy and his political dynasty also includes JFK's brothers, the former Attorney General, Senator for New York and one-time Democratic frontrunner Robert Kennedy, and Edward (Ted) Kennedy, Senator for Massachusetts for 47 years. Joe Kennedy II, son of Robert, served in the House of Representatives for 12 years and his son, Joe Kennedy III, was a member of the House of Representatives for eight years but failed to be elected to the Senate in 2020.

Roosevelt

The two US Presidents with the surname Roosevelt – Theodore and Franklin – were only distantly related (actually fifth cousins) but Franklin then married Theodore's niece, Eleanor Roosevelt, who, after his death, became a delegate to the United Nations. Their sons, James and Franklin Jr, were members of the House of Representatives.

BIGGEST ELECTORAL COLLEGE WINS SINCE 1900

Year	Candidate	Votes
1984	Ronald Reagan	525
1936	Franklin Roosevelt	523
1972	Richard Nixon	520
1980	Ronald Reagan	489
1964	Lyndon Johnson	486
1932	Franklin Roosevelt	472
1956	Dwight Eisenhower	457
1940	Franklin Roosevelt	449
1928	Herbert Hoover	444
1952	Dwight Eisenhower	442
1912	Woodrow Wilson	435
1944	Franklin Roosevelt	432
1988	George HW Bush	426
1920	Warren Harding	404
1932	Calvin Coolidge	382
1996	Bill Clinton	379
1992	Bill Clinton	370
2008	Barack Obama	365
1904	Theodore Roosevelt	336*
2012	Barack Obama	332
1908	William Taft	321†
2020	Joe Biden	306
2016	Donald Trump	304
1948	Harry Truman	303
1960	John F Kennedy	303‡
1968	Richard Nixon	301
2004	George W Bush	286
1976	Jimmy Carter	297
1900	William McKinley	292§
1916	Woodrow Wilson	277
2000	George W Bush	271

Note: From 1912 to 1956, the total number of Electoral College votes was 531.

Since 1964 the total number of Electoral College votes has been 538.

* Total Electoral College votes 446. † Total Electoral College votes 483.

‡ Total Electoral College votes 537. § Total Electoral College votes 447.

TERM LIMIT

Presidents of the USA can serve for a maximum of two terms (plus an additional two years, if these are inherited from a President who has not completed their term) but this restriction only came into force after the four election victories of Franklin Roosevelt. Several Presidents had attempted to win a third term before Roosevelt and all had failed. Roosevelt clinched his third success in 1940 – partly because the world had just embarked on war and America was still fighting its way out of depression – and then claimed a fourth win in 1944, with the war still raging. Republican dissatisfaction with the situation led to the ratification of the 22nd Amendment to the US Constitution in 1951. This changed the rules for all future Presidents, apart from Roosevelt's immediate successor, Harry Truman, who – exempt from the change as he was already in office at the time – remained eligible to win another term in 1952, but declined to run.

RECENT SPEAKERS OF
THE HOUSE OF REPRESENTATIVES

The Speaker of the House of Representatives is elected at the start of each new Congress. Both parties nominate a candidate and, through a roll-call vote, the person securing a majority is appointed. The position involves leading the House, presiding over debates, maintaining order, overseeing the agenda for business and appointing members of committees. The Speaker has always been an elected member of the House (but does not have to be) and sits second in line (after the Vice President) to succeed a sitting President, should the incumbent die or leave office. To date, 52 people have been appointed to the role, some of them re-elected after their first term.

Year	Speaker	State
1940	Samuel T Rayburn D	Texas
1947	Joseph W Martin Jr R	Massachusetts
1949	Samuel T Rayburn D	Texas
1953	Joseph W Martin Jr R	Massachusetts
1955	Samuel T Rayburn D	Texas
1962	John W McCormack D	Massachusetts
1971	Carl B Albert D	Oklahoma
1977	Thomas (Tip) P O'Neill Jr D	Massachusetts
1987	James C Wright Jr D	Texas
1989	Thomas S Foley D	Washington
1995	Newt Gingrich R	Georgia
1999	J Dennis Hastert R	Illinois
2007	Nancy Pelosi D	California
2011	John Boehner R	Ohio
2015	Paul Ryan R	Wisconsin
2019	Nancy Pelosi D	California

THE KITCHEN CABINET

In the 1830s, President Andrew Jackson relied heavily upon the advice of a handful of close political advisors. In a play on words, these advisors, who held more sway than his ministers and other officials, became known as the 'Kitchen Cabinet' to the President's opponents (who also suggested that his actual Cabinet should be known as the 'Parlor Cabinet'). The term has now stuck and 'kitchen cabinet' is widely used to describe any informal group of allies that a political leader depends upon and constantly turns to for advice.

THE PRESIDENTIAL ORDER OF SUCCESSION

In the event that the President of the United States is incapacitated, dies, resigns, is unable to hold office for any reason or is removed from office, they are to be replaced by the holders of the following positions (if eligible), in the following order of precedence, as stipulated in the Presidential Succession Act of 1947, which was signed into law by President Truman.

1 Vice President
2 Speaker of the House of Representatives
3 President Pro Tempore of the Senate
4 Secretary of State
5 Secretary of the Treasury
6 Secretary of Defense
7 Attorney General
8 Secretary of the Interior
9 Secretary of Agriculture
10 Secretary of Commerce
11 Secretary of Labor
12 Secretary of Health and Human Services
13 Secretary of Housing and Urban Development
14 Secretary of Transportation
15 Secretary of Energy
16 Secretary of Education
17 Secretary of Veterans Affairs
18 Secretary of Homeland Security

THE PRESIDENT'S VETO

While US laws are made in Congress, under the terms of the Constitution the President retains a veto and can block the passage of a bill. If the President declines to sign off a new bill, it will be sent back to the part of Congress in which it originated (the House of Representatives or the Senate), where legislators may seek to amend it to accommodate the President's objections. The President must exercise the veto within ten days or the bill automatically becomes law. The veto can be overridden by Congress but only if a two-thirds majority is in favour in both the House and the Senate. If Congress adjourns after sending a bill to the President, the President may take no action (a move known as a 'pocket veto') and, because the bill cannot be returned to Congress, the law simply does not pass.

DEFEATED CANDIDATES IN PRESIDENT ELECTIONS

Year	Candidate	Running Mate
1940	Wendell Willkie R	Charles L McNary
1944	Thomas E Dewey R	John W Bricker
1948	Thomas E Dewey R	Earl Warren
1952	Adlai Stevenson II D	John Sparkman
1956	Adlai Stevenson II D	Estes Kefauver
1960	Richard Nixon R	Henry Cabot Lodge Jr
1964	Barry Goldwater R	William E Miller
1968	Hubert Humphrey D	Edmund Muskie
1972	George McGovern D	Sargent Shriver Jr
1976	Gerald Ford R	Bob Dole
1980	Jimmy Carter D	Walter Mondale
1984	Walter Mondale D	Geraldine Ferraro*
1988	Michael Dukakis D	Lloyd Bentsen
1992	George HW Bush R	Dan Quayle
1996	Bob Dole R	Jack Kemp
2000	Al Gore D	Joe Lieberman
2004	John Kerry D	John Edwards
2008	John McCain R	Sarah Palin
2012	Mitt Romney R	Paul Ryan
2016	Hilary Clinton D	Tim Kaine
2020	Donald Trump R	Mike Pence

* The first woman running mate in a Presidential election.

Note: The above are the main defeated candidates in each race. Only one – Nixon – became President later, with none of the running mates achieving this distinction.

IMPEACHMENT

The action of charging a senior Government official with a crime that makes them unsuitable for office is known as impeachment. While impeachment may take place in other countries, the term is most closely associated with the USA and, in particular, with charges brought against certain Presidents. In such cases, the action is brought by the House of Representatives and the trial takes place in the Senate, with the votes of 67 of the 100 Senators required for a conviction. To date, US Presidents have been impeached on four occasions – Andrew Johnson in 1868, Bill Clinton in 1998–9 and Donald Trump twice, in 2019–20 and 2021. No convictions have followed.

FIRST LADIES OF THE USA

1789 ....Martha Washington	1886 ....Frances Cleveland
1797 ....Abigail Adams	1889 ....Caroline Harrison
1801 ....Martha Randolph*	1892 ....Mary McKee*
1809 ....Dolley Madison	1893 ....Frances Cleveland
1817 ....Elizabeth Monroe	1897 ....Ida McKinley
1825 ....Louisa Adams	1901 ....Edith Roosevelt
1829 ....Emily Donelson*	1909 ....Helen ('Nellie') Taft
1834 ....Sarah Jackson*	1913 ....Ellen Wilson
1838 ....Angelica Van Buren*	1913 ....Margaret Wilson*
1841 ....Anna Taylor	1914 ....Edith Wilson
1841 ....Jane Harrison*	1921 ....Florence Harding
1841 ....Letitia Tyler	1923 ....Grace Coolidge
1842 ....Priscilla Tyler*	1929 ....Lou Hoover
1844 ....Letty Tyler Semple*	1933 ....Eleanor Roosevelt
1844 ....Julia Tyler	1945 ....Elizabeth ('Bess') Truman
1845 ....Sarah Polk	1953 ....Mamie Eisenhower
1849 ....Margaret ('Peggy') Taylor	1961 ....Jacqueline Kennedy
1849 ....Mary 'Betty' Bliss*	1963 . Claudia ('Lady Bird') Johnson
1850 ....Abigail Fillmore	1969 ....Thelma ('Patricia') Nixon
1853 ....Jane Pierce	1974 ....Elizabeth ('Betty') Ford
1857 ....Harriet Lane*	1977 ....Rosalynn Carter
1861 ....Mary Lincoln	1981 ....Nancy Reagan
1865 ....Eliza Johnson	1989 ....Barbara Bush
1865 .....Martha Johnson Patterson*	1993 ....Hillary Clinton
1869 ....Julia Grant	2001 ....Laura Bush
1877 ....Lucy Hayes	2009 ....Michelle Obama
1881 ....Lucretia Garfield	2017 ....Melania Trump
1881 ....Mary McElroy*	2021 ....Jill Biden
1885 ....Rose Cleveland*	

* Not spouse: the role of First Lady is traditionally filled by the spouse of the President but occasionally has been taken on by other family members.
Note: Some sources also list as First Ladies two spouses who died before their husbands took office – Rachel Jackson (1828) and Ellen Arthur (1880).

VOTE TOTALS IN THE 2020 PRESIDENTIAL ELECTION

Joe Biden 81,268,924 (highest ever) · Donald Trump 74,216,154

THE ELECTORAL COLLEGE

Who becomes the President of the United States is not decided by a simple national vote. Instead, votes are tallied state by state, with the winner of the popular vote in each state receiving the total number of votes the state has been allocated in what is known as the Electoral College.* The Electoral College has a total of 538 votes, which are shared among the states as outlined below. A candidate who wins 270 or more of these votes – a simple majority – is declared the winner. While the result of a Presidential Election is often called by the media on election night, the result is not official until the Electoral College meets several weeks later and electors from each state personally deliver their results, which must then be certified by Congress.

State	Votes	State	Votes	State	Votes
Alabama	9	Kentucky	8	North Dakota	3
Alaska	3	Louisiana	8	Ohio	17
Arizona	11	Maine	4	Oklahoma	7
Arkansas	6	Maryland	10	Oregon	8
California	54	Massachusetts	11	Pennsylvania	19
Colorado	10	Michigan	15	Rhode Island	4
Connecticut	7	Minnesota	10	South Carolina	9
Delaware	3	Mississippi	6	South Dakota	3
District of Columbia	3	Missouri	10	Tennessee	11
Florida	30	Montana	4	Texas	40
Georgia	16	Nebraska	5	Utah	6
Hawaii	4	Nevada	6	Vermont	3
Idaho	4	New Hampshire	4	Virginia	13
Illinois	19	New Jersey	14	Washington	12
Indiana	11	New Mexico	5	West Virginia	4
Iowa	6	New York	28	Wisconsin	10
Kansas	6	North Carolina	16	Wyoming	3

Note: Figures apply from the 2024 Presidential Election.
* Maine and Nebraska give some votes to the winner of the overall state popular vote and others according to how votes have been cast in Congressional districts.

A NATURAL-BORN PRESIDENT

The first President actually to be born as a US citizen was the country's eighth, Martin Van Buren. All his predecessors were born when the country was a colony of the United Kingdom and were, technically, British subjects.

POLITICAL CURRENCY

The USA's banknotes and coins serve as a constant reminder of the country's political history, with images of past Presidents and other notable figures on one side and important buildings and other images on the other.

Denomination	Person	Image
Coins		
1¢ (penny)	Abraham Lincoln	Union Shield
5¢ (nickel)	Thomas Jefferson	Monticello*
10¢ (dime)	Franklin Roosevelt	Torch, olive and oak branches†
25¢ (quarter)	George Washington	National parks (images vary)‡
50¢ (half dollar)	John F Kennedy	Presidential seal§
Banknotes		
$1	George Washington	Seal of the United States
$2	Thomas Jefferson	Declaration of Independence Signing
$5	Abraham Lincoln	Lincoln Memorial
$10	Alexander Hamilton	US Treasury
$20	Andrew Jackson	The White House
$50	Ulysses S Grant	US Capitol
$100	Benjamin Franklin	Independence Hall, Philadelphia

* Jefferson's plantation home in Virginia.

† Representing liberty, peace, and strength and independence, respectively.

‡ Other, limited-run 25¢ coins are also minted, depicting important national sites and celebrated American women.

§ Now generally minted as collectables. $1 coins are also still minted for collectors, with varying imagery.

PRESIDENTS' DAY

The third Monday in February every year is a US public holiday generally known as Presidents' Day. However, the official title is Washington's Birthday, as the event fell on that day – 22 February – when initiated back in the 1880s (attempts to change the name, because the holiday falls on a different date each year, so far have come to nothing). These days, the holiday is seen as a double celebration, marking the birth of both Washington and Abraham Lincoln (on 12 February), and also honouring collectively the lives and service of all the former Presidents of the country.

WHO'S PRESIDENT?

In the event that a Presidential election ends with no candidate gaining an overall majority in the Electoral College, the winner is selected from among the top three candidates by a vote in the House of Representatives. The Vice President is then chosen by the Senate from the remaining two candidates. Only once has this situation occurred – when John Quincy Adams became President after the 1824 election despite his main rival, Andrew Jackson, receiving more votes in the Electoral College and topping the popular vote.

PRESIDENTS AWARDED THE NOBEL PEACE PRIZE

1906 Theodore Roosevelt
'for his role in bringing to an end the bloody war recently waged between two of the world's great powers, Japan and Russia'

1920 Woodrow Wilson
'for his role as founder of the League of Nations'

2002 Jimmy Carter
'for his decades of untiring effort to find peaceful solutions to international conflicts, to advance democracy and human rights, and to promote economic and social development'

2009 Barack Obama
'for his extraordinary efforts to strengthen international diplomacy and cooperation between peoples'

Note: One US Vice President – Al Gore in 2007 – has also been a recipient.

HANCOCK'S FINEST HOUR

The first delegate to sign the US Declaration of Independence in 1776 was John Hancock, President of the Continental Congress, which drew up the document. A Harvard graduate and a Boston merchant, Hancock was a leading figure in the Revolutionary War and later served as Governor of Massachusetts, but his role in history is defined by the bold autograph he left with a flourish on one of America's most important pieces of paper: his name has become a common byname for a personal signature of any kind.

PRIMARY OR CAUCUS?

Presidential election candidates for the major parties are chosen through a state-by-state series of contests known either as primaries or caucuses.*

Primaries

A primary is a straightforward election and maybe 'closed' or 'open'. Closed primaries restrict the right to vote to declared party members, while open primaries enable the general public, irrespective of any party affiliation, to take part. For Democratic primaries, a form of proportional representation is used to share out the number of delegates that have been allocated to the state among the candidates who poll the most, while in most Republican primaries, the winner of the vote simply acquires all the delegates.

Caucuses

In contrast to a primary, a caucus requires voters to attend a meeting before voting. This means that only committed voters generally take part. The rules vary between the two parties and among the states holding caucuses but the basic principle is as follows. During these meetings, voters arrange themselves in groups to show their support for a particular candidate and to try to secure a good share of delegates for them, with speeches made to attract wavering voters to their side. If a group fails to attract 15 per cent of the total attendance, its candidate is eliminated and its members can transfer their allegiance to another candidate, if they so wish. In recent years, the number of caucuses has been reduced by both parties, in favour of the simpler primary.

Note: What these events actually do is choose delegates who pledge to cast votes for the favoured candidates at a later national convention. In the 1980s, the Democratic Party complicated matters by adding a national group of 'superdelegates' to the mix. This collection of senior party figures now contribute their votes to the final tally at the convention. A similar, but more limited, system is used by the Republican Party.

THE DESIGNATED SURVIVOR

Whenever the President, Vice President and other key members of the administration all attend a major event – such as the State of the Union speech at the Capitol – one member of the Cabinet is instructed to take refuge in a secure, undisclosed location in case those attending are killed through a hostile attack or other incident. The 'designated survivor' can then become Acting President and governance of the country can continue.

99

THE PRESIDENTIAL OATHS

The President
'I do solemnly swear (or affirm) that I will faithfully execute the Office of President of the United States, and will to the best of my ability, preserve, protect and defend the Constitution of the United States.'

The Vice President*
'I do solemnly swear (or affirm) that I will support and defend the Constitution of the United States against all enemies, foreign and domestic; that I will bear true faith and allegiance to the same; that I take this obligation freely, without any mental reservation or purpose of evasion; and that I will well and faithfully discharge the duties of the office on which I am about to enter: So help me God.'

*The same oath taken by Congressmen and some Federal employees.

THE STATE OF THE UNION ADDRESS

The US Constitution stipulates that the President 'shall from time to time give to the Congress Information of the State of the Union' – hence the important address that the President now delivers to Congress once a year.

The tradition was begun by George Washington in 1790 and continued by his successor, John Adams.

The third President, Thomas Jefferson, not noted as a public speaker, declined to deliver the speech in person and forwarded instead a written report. It wasn't until 1913 that the oral format was revived by Woodrow Wilson.

The address is given in the House of Representatives and, until 1934, annually in December. Since that time, it has been heard on various dates in January or early February.

The speech was known simply as the 'Annual Message' until 1947 when, under its present name, the first televised address was delivered by Harry Truman.

The content of the speech has changed over the years. Detailed reports on the economy were once part of the ritual but today separate written summaries cover this subject and so the speech has become instead an exercise in promoting and building support for the President's agenda – finely honed, of course, for the enormous television audience.

THE FILIBUSTER PROBLEM

A filibuster, historically, was a pirate who roamed the Caribbean, raiding and plundering Spanish colonies, during the 17th century. The name is derived from the same linguistic roots as 'freebooter'.

Politically, a filibuster is a wrecking device, used to delay or block legislation, particularly in the US Senate. It refers to when Senators who oppose certain legislation, speak for so long in a debate that the bill does not pass because time runs out. These days, they don't always even have to speak: the mere threat of talking out a bill may cause a blockage.

There is, however, a safeguard that, in theory, prevents this from happening constantly. Since 1917, Senate rules have stated that, if enough Senators object to the use of the filibuster then it can be terminated and a vote can be forced – 'cloture' being the technical terminology. Initially, this threshold was set at two-thirds of the Senate membership (67 Senators) but, in 1975, the number was reduced to three-fifths (60 Senators).

Unfortunately, even this safeguard has proven inadequate at times, particularly in recent years. Increasing partisanship in the Senate now often makes it impossible to reach the cloture threshold, leading to new calls for the removal of the filibuster in its entirety.

PRESIDENTS ELECTED WITHOUT WINNING THE POPULAR VOTE

Because US Presidents are elected via the Electoral College system and not by the number of votes received nationally (the popular vote), it is possible for candidates to be elected despite not being the favoured choice of voters. This has happened four times, with the declared winners all Republicans.

Year	Elected President	Vote%	Defeated Rival	Vote%
1876	Rutherford Hayes	48.0	Samuel Tilden	51.0
1888	Benjamin Harrison	47.8	Grover Cleveland	48.7
2000	George W Bush	47.9	Al Gore	48.4
2016	Donald Trump	46.0	Hillary Clinton	48.1

Note: In 1824, John Quincy Adams was elected without winning the Electoral College or the popular vote. See *Who's President?* (p. 98).

PRESIDENTIAL LIBRARIES

Documents and artefacts relating to a Presidency are curated in 14 Presidential Libraries operated by the National Archives and Records Administration (NARA). Visitors can view exhibits and learn more about each administration, while archive material is made available to researchers.

President	Location of Library
Herbert Hoover	West Branch, Iowa
Franklin Roosevelt	Hyde Park, New York
Harry Truman	Independence, Missouri
Dwight Eisenhower	Abilene, Kansas
John F Kennedy	Boston, Massachusetts
Lyndon Johnson	Austin, Texas
Richard Nixon	Yorba Linda, California
Gerald Ford	Ann Arbor, Michigan*
Jimmy Carter	Atlanta, Georgia
Ronald Reagan	Simi Valley, California
George HW Bush	College Station, Texas
Bill Clinton	Little Rock, Arkansas
George Bush	Dallas, Texas
Barack Obama	No physical libary†

* Separate museum at Grand Rapids, Michigan.

† Plans for digital access to materials; a new privately-run museum site is under construction in Chicago, Illinois.

A FIRESIDE CHAT

Between 1933 and 1944, President Franklin Roosevelt became known for a series of informal radio broadcasts, designed to lift the mood of the nation and garner support for his plans during the Great Depression and the early years of the Second World War. These broadcasts, direct from the White House, were dubbed 'Fireside Chats' by the CBS executive Harry Butcher and allowed the President to explain often quite complicated issues – such as his New Deal – in simple layman's terms. The broadcasts – 30 in total over the 11 years – were largely prepared by a team of advisors but Roosevelt – well aware that this powerful new medium allowed him to speak directly to the people, without the mediation of the press – was, of course, personally responsible for their reassuring, warm, conversational delivery.

AMENDMENTS TO THE US CONSTITUTION

No.	Summary	Year
1st	Freedom of religion, speech, the press, assembly and to petition	1791
2nd	Right to bear arms.	1791
3rd	No quartering of Government troops in private homes	1791
4th	No unreasonable search and seizure of property	1791
5th	Right to fair trial, to be not tried twice on same facts and to remain silent; no seizure of property without compensation	1791
6th	Right to swift, informed trial by one's peers, to confront and compel testimony from witnesses, to have legal representation	1791
7th	Right to have civil cases tried by jury	1791
8th	Prohibition of excessive bail, fines and punishments	1791
9th	List of rights included in the Constitution is not exhaustive	1791
10th	All powers not designated to the United States are assigned to the States or the people	1791
11th	Protection of states from legal action by citizens of another state	1795
12th	Procedure for the election of the President and Vice President	1804
13th	Abolition of slavery	1865
14th	Rights of US citizens; prohibition from office for insurrection; no liability for the United States for financial claims resulting from aiding insurrection, or the emancipation of slaves	1868
15th	Right to vote irrespective of race, colour or previous servitude	1870
16th	Right of Congress to collect taxes on incomes	1913
17th	Rules for the election of Senators to the US Senate	1913
18th	Prohibition of the manufacture, sale or transportation of alcoholic drinks	1919
19th	Right to vote for all sexes	1920
20th	Terms of office of elected officials and provision for the death of a President Elect	1933
21st	Repeal of the 18th Amendment and removal of prohibition	1933
22nd	Limitation of Presidential service to two terms or ten years	1951
23rd	Right to vote for District of Columbia citizens in Presidential elections	1961
24th	Right to vote in Presidential and Congressional elections not to be denied for failure to pay any tax	1964
25th	Procedure for the removal of a President from office	1967
26th	Right to vote for those aged 18 and older	1971
27th	Rule on the compensation of Senators and Representatives	1992

Note: 1st–10th Amendments constitute the Bill of Rights.

THE RESURRECTED PRESIDENT

In 1991, the remains of America's 12th President, Zachary Taylor, who died in 1850, were exhumed for analysis, to see if rumours that he had been poisoned by arsenic (thus suggesting that he had been the first President to be assassinated) were true. Sadly, for conspiracy theorists, they were not.

NUMBER OF SENATORS
AND REPRESENTATIVES PER STATE

The total number of Senators elected to serve in the US Senate is 100, with each state allocated two Senators. The total number of Representatives (Congressmen/women) serving in the House of Representatives is 435, with each state given an allocation that is adjusted according to the state's population size after each national census (every ten years), although all states are guaranteed at least one Representative. Following the 2020 census, the allocation per state was as follows:

Alabama 7	Louisiana 6	Ohio 15
Alaska 1	Maine 2	Oklahoma 5
Arizona 9	Maryland 8	Oregon 6
Arkansas 4	Massachusetts 9	Pennsylvania 17
California 52	Michigan 13	Rhode Island 2
Colorado 8	Minnesota 8	South Carolina 7
Connecticut 5	Mississippi 4	South Dakota 1
Delaware 1	Missouri 8	Tennessee 9
Florida 28	Montana 2	Texas 38
Georgia 14	Nebraska 3	Utah 4
Hawaii 2	Nevada 4	Vermont 1
Idaho 2	New Hampshire 2	Virginia 11
Illinois 17	New Jersey 12	Washington 10
Indiana 9	New Mexico 3	West Virginia 2
Iowa 4	New York 26	Wisconsin 8
Kansas 4	North Carolina 14	Wyoming 1
Kentucky 6	North Dakota 1	Total 435

THE ORIGINAL COMEBACK KID

The only President to reclaim office after election defeat is Grover Cleveland.

PRESIDENTIAL DEBATES

The US tradition of televising live debates between the principal contenders in a presidential election dates back to 1960. On 26 September that year, Republican candidate Richard Nixon and his Democratic rival, John F Kennedy, squared off in a programme broadcast by CBS from Chicago.

Although three further debates followed, this first encounter was generally considered to be the most decisive and influential, testifying to the visual impact of television – the clean-shaven, tanned, relaxed Kennedy was thought to have outshone the pale, stubbly, sweaty Nixon, who had recently spent time in hospital and was reportedly suffering with a fever on the night.

Despite the ground-breaking nature of the 1960 events, it was another 16 years before the next presidential debate took place because the incumbent Presidents Johnson and Nixon declined to share airtime with their opponents.

The format resumed with the challenger Jimmy Carter debating with President Gerald Ford in 1976 and has continued in every election since, although the format has varied from debate to debate.

THE UNELECTED PRESIDENT

The only President not elected President or Vice President is Gerald Ford. He was appointed Vice President by Richard Nixon after the resignation of Spiro Agnew and then assumed the Presidency when Nixon himself resigned.

A RABBIT'S-EYE VIEW

The 2018 book *A Day in the Life of the Vice President* is a deep burrow into the day-to-day activities of the then VP, Mike Pence. This important work was actually written by Pence's daughter, Charlotte, and published with illustrations by his wife, Karen – clearly two people with close-up experience of life at the top of Government. Refreshingly however, this was not a warts-and-all exposé but rather an off-beat take on the Pence family's experience as seen through the eyes of their pet rabbit, one Marlon Bundo, the black-and-white so-called BOTUS, or Bunny of the United States. The book proved successful enough to generate two spin-off titles, handily earning children's charities some very useful bucks and rather a lot of doe.

WINNING PRESIDENTIAL CAMPAIGN SLOGANS

Year	Slogan	Candidate
1948	*I'm Just Wild About Harry*	Harry Truman
1952	*I Like Ike*	Dwight Eisenhower
1956	*I Still Like Ike*	Dwight Eisenhower
1960	*A Time for Greatness*	John F Kennedy
1964	*All the Way with LBJ*	Lyndon Johnson
1968	*This Time, Vote Like Your Whole World Depended on It*	Richard Nixon
1972	*Nixon Now More Than Ever*	Richard Nixon
1976	*Not Just Peanuts*	Jimmy Carter
1980	*Let's Make America Great Again*	Ronald Reagan
1984	*It's Morning Again in America*	Ronald Reagan
1988	*Kinder, Gentler Nation*	George HW Bush
1992	*Putting People First*	Bill Clinton
1996	*Building a Bridge to the 21st Century*	Bill Clinton
2000	*Compassionate Conservatism*	George W Bush
2004	*A Safer World and a More Hopeful America*	George W Bush
2008	*Change We Can Believe In*	Barack Obama
2012	*Forward*	Barack Obama
2016	*Make America Great Again*	Donald Trump
2020	*Build Back Better*	Joe Biden

Note: Other slogans were also used by some candidates during their campaigns.

FEDERAL GOVERNMENT V STATE GOVERNMENT

The Federal Government of the USA has certain national powers but many of the country's laws are actually derived from State Governments and apply only locally. Each State Government mirrors the Federal Government in having three distinct branches – the Executive Branch (led by the elected Governor), the Legislative Branch (mostly made up of two elected law-making bodies, usually known as the Senate and the House of Representatives), and the Judicial Branch (headed up by a Supreme Court).

THE UNICAMERAL STATE

All US states have two law-making assemblies except one. In Nebraska, there is a Senate but no 'House of Representatives'-style second chamber.

INDEPENDENCE OR DEATH

The USA declared its independence from Britain on 4 July 1776. Strangely, the same date, 50 years later, saw the death of two of its earliest Presidents, John Adams and Thomas Jefferson. A third US President, James Monroe, also died on Independence Day five years later. Only one President was born on that celebrated day, however: the 30th, Calvin Coolidge, in 1872.

RECENT US SECRETARIES OF STATE

1933 .... Cordell Hull	1982 .... George Shultz
1944 .... Edward Stettinius	1989 .... James Baker
1945 .... James Byrnes	1992 .... Lawrence Eagleburger
1947 .... George Marshall	1993 .... Warren Christopher
1949 .... Dean Acheson	1997 .... Madeleine Albright
1953 .... John Foster Dulles	2001 .... Colin Powell
1959 .... Christian Herter	2005 .... Condoleezza Rice
1961 .... Dean Rusk	2009 .... Hilary Clinton
1969 .... William Rogers	2013 .... John Kerry
1973 .... Henry Kissinger	2017 .... Rex Tillerson
1977 .... Cyrus Vance	2018 .... Mike Pompeo
1980 .... Edmund Muskie	2021 .... Antony Blinken
1981 .... Alexander Haig	

Note: The Secretary of State is effectively the head of foreign affairs.

EXECUTIVE ORDERS

While the US President is at the mercy of Congress when it comes to pursuing an agenda and making new laws, some limited actions can be achieved through what is known as an executive order – effectively, an instruction to those parts of the US system directly under the President's control to enforce existing laws in a particular way. This action cannot be overturned by Congress unless it is deemed beyond the authority of the President as head of state, Commander-in-Chief, chief law enforcement officer and head of the Executive Branch. Many executive orders deal with mundane details of governance, but others have been more controversial and have been criticised for being used to subvert existing laws or to allow the President to introduce measures not supported or voted for by Congress.

THE RESOLUTE DESK

A noted, elegant feature of the President's Oval Office is the Resolute Desk, an ornate desk made from the oak timbers of *HMS Resolute* – a ship abandoned when trapped in ice in the 1850s, after failing in its mission to find the lost Arctic explorer Sir John Franklin. The desk was presented to President Rutherford Hayes by Queen Victoria in 1880. It was first relocated to the Oval Office from the main White House under John F Kennedy and when his successor, Lyndon Johnson, replaced it with another desk, it went on display at the Smithsonian Museum in Washington until being brought back into executive action by Jimmy Carter in 1977. With the exception of George HW Bush, who chose to use a different desk for most of his time in the White House, it has been the place of work of all Presidents since Carter.

DOUBLE SIGNATORIES

The US Declaration of Independence from the United Kingdom was signed by 56 men in 1776. Among the signatories were John Adams, Thomas Jefferson and Samuel Adams (after whom the beer brand was named). In 1787, the US Constitution was drawn up and signed by 39 delegates, including George Washington, James Madison and Alexander Hamilton. However, only the following six men were signatories to both documents.

George Clymer (*Pennsylvania*) · Benjamin Franklin (*Pennsylvania*)
Robert Morris (*Pennsylvania*) · George Read (*Delaware*)
Roger Sherman (*Connecticut*) · James Wilson (*Pennsylvania*)

A SECOND WHITE HOUSE

The official residence of the US Vice President is Number One Observatory Circle, a 19th-century, graceful, white-painted property a couple of miles from the White House, that was refurbished for this purpose in the 1970s. Walter Mondale and his family were the first to live in the premises – previously VPs lived in their own homes – although his predecessor, Nelson Rockefeller, had sometimes used the house for entertaining. The US Naval Observatory, on whose land the building sits, remains operational as an astronomical centre. The Vice President's Ceremonial Office is located separately, however, in the Eisenhower Executive Office Building in the White House grounds, and the VP also has an office within the West Wing.

A CALENDAR OF
PRESIDENTIAL PRIMARIES AND CAUCUSES

Early February
Iowa *C*

Mid February
New Hampshire

Late February
Nevada *C*
South Carolina

Early March*
Alabama
American Samoa *C*
Arkansas
California
Colorado
Maine
Massachusetts
Minnesota
North Carolina
Oklahoma
Tennessee
Texas
Utah
Vermont
Virginia

Mid March
Arizona
Florida

Idaho
Illinois
Michigan
Mississippi
Missouri
North Dakota *C*
Northern Mariana
Islands *C*
Washington

Early April
Wisconsin

Mid April
Alaska
Wyoming *C*

Late April
Ohio

Early May
Kansas

Mid May
Nebraska
Oregon

Late May
Hawaii

Early June
District of Columbia
Georgia
Guam *C*
Indiana
Maryland
Montana
New Mexico
Pennsylvania
Rhode Island
South Dakota
US Virgin Islands *C*
West Virginia

Late June
Kentucky
New York

Early July
Delaware
New Jersey

Mid July
Louisiana
Puerto Rico

Mid August
Connecticut

C · caucus.

* Known as 'Super Tuesday' because of the large number of states holding primaries or caucuses on this day – each wanting to exert some early influence in the race for the Presidential nomination.

Note: Dates based on Democratic primaries and caucuses in 2020 when there were few Republican events. These dates may change from election to election. The Republicans' dates are usually broadly similar but do vary in some instances.

THE CONFEDERATE STATES

In 1860–1, the 11 southern states of the USA listed below seceded from Union after decades of disagreements with their northern counterparts over numerous issues, but primarily slavery. The new (never recognised as sovereign) nation they created was known as the Confederacy and had its own flag, currency and postage stamps. Jefferson Davis of Mississippi, a former US Congressman and Senator, was elected President, with Alexander Stephens of Georgia as his Vice President. The capital city was initially Montgomery, Alabama, but was soon moved to Richmond, Virginia. This secession of the Confederate states ultimately led to the American Civil War, which was won by the Union (northern states) under President Abraham Lincoln and, in 1865, the Confederacy ceased to exist.

Alabama · Arkansas · Florida · Georgia · Louisiana · Mississippi
North Carolina · South Carolina · Tennessee · Texas · Virginia

Note: The Confederacy also claimed the states of Missouri and Kentucky – hence
the 13 stars on the Confederate flag – but these states always officially remained
part of the Union.

THE CAPITOL

The white, neo-classical Capitol building in Washington, DC, is the home of the US House of Representatives and the Senate.

The building was designed by an amateur architect named Dr William Thornton, with work beginning in 1793 when George Washington laid the foundation stone. However, the current structure bears only a passing resemblance to Thornton's design, as other architects – including the White House architect James Hoban – were brought in later to supervise its completion.

Congress took up residence in 1800 even though the original structure was not finished until 1826.

Capacity issues soon demanded expansion – new northern and southern wings and the now-familiar higher dome, in the style of the dome of St Peter's in Rome, were added by the architect Thomas Ustick Walter. The eastern facade was slightly extended in the 1960s.

Other buildings now constructed alongside house the Supreme Court, the Library of Congress and more office accommodation.

THE DECLARATION OF INDEPENDENCE (EXTRACT)

'We hold these truths to be self-evident, that all men are created equal, that they are endowed by their Creator with certain unalienable Rights, that among these are Life, Liberty and the pursuit of Happiness. That to secure these rights, Governments are instituted among Men, deriving their just powers from the consent of the governed. That whenever any Form of Government becomes destructive of these ends, it is the Right of the People to alter or to abolish it, and to institute new Government, laying its foundation on such principles and organizing its powers in such form, as to them shall seem most likely to effect their Safety and Happiness.'

COMMON ABBREVIATIONS IN US POLITICS

ATF	Bureau of Alcohol, Tobacco, Firearms and Explosives
CDC	Centers for Disease Control and Prevention
CIA	Central Intelligence Agency
DHS	Department of Homeland Security
DOE	Department of Energy
DOI	Department of Interior
DOJ	Department of Justice
DOL	Department of Labor
DOT	Department of Transportation
EPA	Environmental Protection Agency
FBI	Federal Bureau of Investigation
FDA	Food and Drug Administration
FEC	Federal Election Commission
FEMA	Federal Emergency Management Agency
FLOTUS	First Lady of the United States
GOP	Grand Old Party (Republican Party)
HUD	Department of Housing and Urban Development
ICE	Immigration and Customs Enforcement
IRS	Internal Revenue Service
LOC	Library of Congress
NIH	National Institutes of Health
NSA	National Security Agency
NSC	National Security Council
OSG	Office of the Surgeon General
POTUS	President of the United States
SCOTUS	Supreme Court of the United States

MY COUSIN, THE PRESIDENT

First Lady Barbara Bush was born into the Presidency, it could be said. The 14th President, Franklin Pierce, was her fourth cousin four times removed.

SECOND NAMES OF US PRESIDENTS

John *Quincy* Adams
William *Henry* Harrison
James *Knox* Polk
Hiram Ulysses Grant*
Rutherford *Birchard* Hayes
James *Abram* Garfield
Chester *Alan* Arthur
Stephen Grover Cleveland
William *Howard* Taft
Thomas Woodrow Wilson
Warren *Gamaliel* Harding
John Calvin Coolidge
Herbert *Clark* Hoover
Franklin *Delano* Roosevelt

Harry *S* Truman†
Dwight *David* Eisenhower
John *Fitzgerald* Kennedy
Lyndon *Baines* Johnson
Richard *Milhous* Nixon
Gerald *Rudolph* Ford‡
Jimmy *Earl* Carter
Ronald *Wilson* Reagan
George *Herbert Walker* Bush
Bill *Jefferson* Clinton
George *Walker* Bush
Barack *Hussein* Obama
Donald *John* Trump
Joe *Robinette* Biden

* 'Ulysses S Grant' was an error made during enrolment at West Point that stuck.
† The middle initial was bestowed to honour both Truman's grandfathers but didn't actually stand for anything.
‡ Birth name was Leslie Lynch King.

CONGRESSIONAL QUORUM

Under the Constitution of the USA, a simple majority of members of the House of Representatives and the Senate must be present in order for business to be conducted. With the total House membership totalling 435, the quorum is therefore 218; with 100 members of the Senate, the quorum is 51. In practice, this doesn't preclude debate taking place, as it is always assumed that a quorum is in place, but, occasionally, politicians may try to buy some time – perhaps to allow informal discussions to overcome a particular problem – by initiating a 'quorum call'. This involves a roll-call of members by the clerk. If there is no quorum, members are summoned to attend the Chamber in sufficient number to allow business to continue.

CAMP DAVID

The US President's country residence is Camp David, a former retreat for Federal employees and their families located in Catoctin Mountain Park, Maryland, on the fringe of the Blue Mountains, around 65 miles northwest of Washington, DC. Franklin Roosevelt was the first President to make use of this facility in 1942, naming it USS Shangri La, and designing the main lodge after his own winter vacation home in Warm Springs, Georgia. The following year, Winston Churchill became the first of many foreign leaders to visit. The 200-acre site was renamed Camp David by President Dwight Eisenhower – after his five-year-old grandson – in 1953, although the official name of residence is actually Naval Support Facility Thurmont.

EVERYONE'S PRESIDENT

The only President to be elected unanimously was the very first, George Washington, who took all the 69 votes available in the Electoral College of 1789. The feat was nearly repeated in 1820 when President James Monroe – running almost unopposed – was re-elected with only one vote against (a representative from New Hampshire voted instead for John Quincy Adams).

ROE V WADE

In 1973, the Supreme Court ruled on a landmark case known as Roe v Wade. The subject was a woman's right to have an abortion and whether individual states had the power to prevent this. 'Jane Roe' was a pseudonym for Norma McCorvey, who was challenging Henry Wade, the district attorney of her county in Texas, over this matter. The Court's decision, in favour of Roe and based on the constitutional right to privacy of women, with some caveats relating to pregnancy term limits, dictated US abortion law for nearly 50 years. It was overturned by a Supreme Court with a conservative majority in 2022 when it ruled that a ban on abortions in Mississippi after 15 weeks was legal. Other states then swiftly moved to enforce their own new laws.

AN EASTER TREAT

A popular Washington tradition – established by President Rutherford Hayes in 1878 – is the children's Egg Roll held at Easter on the White House lawn.

THE FBI AND THE CIA

The FBI

The Federal Bureau of Investigation (FBI) is the main investigative agency of the USA and is part of the Executive Branch of the US Federal Government, reporting to the Attorney General.

It was founded in 1908 under Attorney General Charles Bonaparte – a grandnephew of Napoleon – and adopted the name the Bureau of Investigation a year later.

The Bureau was substantially remodelled and refocused from 1924, when the agency's best-known director, J Edgar Hoover, was appointed by the Attorney General Harlan F Stone. Hoover went on to lead the organisation until 1972. Appointment to this role is now made by the President.

The agency – renamed the Federal Bureau of Investigation in 1935 – has its headquarters in Washington, DC, and, although its remit extends to only domestic matters, it also has offices in other countries to enable easy interchange of intelligence internationally.

Crimes investigated by the FBI range from organised crime and terrorism to cybercrime and money laundering. The agency also takes the lead on counterintelligence domestically.

The CIA

With its headquarters in Langley, Virginia, the Central Intelligence Agency (CIA) is the USA's main foreign intelligence and counter-intelligence agency and is part of the Executive Branch of the US Federal Government.

It was founded in 1947 as an independent civilian agency to replace the Office of Strategic Services (OSS), which had provided intelligence during the Second World War and was the first co-ordinated security service operation in US history (previously the Department of State, the FBI and the military worked separately and often declined to share information).

The CIA is overseen by the National Security Council (NSC), which advises the President on security matters.

By law, the Agency is forbidden to conduct operations against US persons (including citizens, corporations and legal immigrants) but it does have a domestic unit that works alongside the FBI.

The official seal of the CIA incorporates an eagle (said to be for alertness), a shield (for defence) and a compass rose (signifying the Agency's international remit).

SOME PREVIOUS JOBS OF US PRESIDENTS

As shown below, the profession favoured by most US Presidents before entering politics is law. Numerous Presidents had more than one earlier job and many also served in the military in addition to the occupations listed.

Acting
Ronald Reagan

Architecture
Thomas Jefferson

Education
James Garfield · Chester Arthur
Woodrow Wilson · Lyndon Johnson

Engineering
Herbert Hoover

Farming
John Adams · Thomas Jefferson
Harry Truman · Jimmy Carter

Football Coaching
Gerald Ford

Haberdashery
Harry Truman

Law
John Adams · Thomas Jefferson
Andrew Jackson · Abraham Lincoln

Grover Cleveland · William Taft
Woodrow Wilson · Calvin Coolidge
Franklin Roosevelt · Richard Nixon
Gerald Ford · Bill Clinton
Barack Obama · Joe Biden

Military
George Washington
Ulysses S Grant
Dwight Eisenhower

Modelling
Gerald Ford

Sheriff*
Grover Cleveland

Surveying
George Washington

Tailoring
Andrew Johnson

Writing/Journalism
Theodore Roosevelt
John F Kennedy

* And hangman.

VOTE FOR CONVICT NO. 9653

In 1920, the committed socialist Eugene Debs ran for President for the fifth time and won nearly a million votes, despite being in prison in Atlanta at the time, convicted of charges relating to a speech he had made against war.

SOME NICKNAMES OF US PRESIDENTS

Nickname	President
American Cincinnatus	George Washington
Big Chief	William Taft
Colossus of Independence	John Adams
Comeback Kid	Bill Clinton
Dubya	George W Bush
Dude President	Chester Arthur
Gipper	Ronald Reagan
Great Communicator	Ronald Reagan
Great Engineer	Herbert Hoover
Handsome Frank	Franklin Pierce
Hero of Appomattox	Ulysses S Grant
His Accidency	John Tyler
His Fraudulency	Rutherford Hayes
His Obstinacy	Grover Cleveland
Honest Abe	Abraham Lincoln
Human Iceberg	Benjamin Harrison
Ike	Dwight Eisenhower
Last Cocked Hat	James Monroe
LBJ	Lyndon Johnson
Little Magician	Martin Van Buren
Old Hickory	Andrew Jackson
Old Public Functionary	James Buchanan
Old Rough and Ready	Zachary Taylor
Old Sink or Swim	John Adams
Peanut Farmer	Jimmy Carter
Rail-Splitter	Abraham Lincoln
Sage of Monticello	Thomas Jefferson
Schoolmaster	Woodrow Wilson
Silent Cal	Calvin Coolidge
Slick Willie	Bill Clinton
Sphinx	Franklin Roosevelt
Ten-Cent Jimmy	James Buchanan
Tennessee Tailor	Andrew Johnson
Tricky Dick	Richard Nixon
Trust Buster	Theodore Roosevelt
Young Hickory	Franklin Pierce

DISTRICT OF COLUMBIA

In 1790, a 100-square-mile plot of land – later named the District of Columbia, or DC for short – was set aside by the US Congress to become the home of the US Federal Government. The area incorporated land released for the purpose by the states of Maryland and Virginia alongside the Potomac River. The city of Washington was constructed within the site but has since has expanded to consume the whole territory. Governance of DC – which is not one of the United States – is handled by an elected mayor.

THE BACHELOR PRESIDENT

Only one US President never married: the 15th, James Buchanan, who remained a lifelong bachelor. His niece, Harriet Lane, served as his First Lady.

THE YOUNGEST AND OLDEST PRESIDENTS

President	Age*
Youngest	
1 ....Theodore Roosevelt	42 years 322 days
2 ....John F Kennedy	43 years 236 days
3 ....Bill Clinton	46 years 154 days
4 ....Ulysses S Grant	46 years 311 days
5 ....Barack Obama	47 years 169 days
6 ....Grover Cleveland	47 years 351 days
7 ....Franklin Pierce	48 years 101 days
8 ....James Garfield	49 years 105 days
9 ....James Polk	49 years 123 days
10 ......Millard Fillmore	50 years 183 days
Oldest	
36 ......John Adams	61 years 125 days
37 ......Andrew Jackson	61 years 354 days
38 ......Dwight Eisenhower	62 years 98 days
39 ......Zachary Taylor	64 years 100 days
40 ......George HW Bush	64 years 222 days
41 ......James Buchanan	65 years 315 days
42 ......William Harrison	68 years 23 days
43 ......Ronald Reagan	69 years 349 days
44 ......Donald Trump	70 years 220 days
45 ......Joe Biden	78 years 61 days

* At time of first inauguration.

MAJORITY AND MINORITY LEADERS

The Senate Majority Leader is the leader of the largest party in the Senate. As the office entails taking responsibility for the legislative programme and the time available for debate, the holder wields a great deal of power. The Senate Minority Leader is the leader of the second largest party and has much less influence. In the House of Representatives, the Majority Leader has less power than the equivalent in the Senate, being subordinate to the Speaker of the House, who generally comes from the same party. The role is therefore usually restricted to promoting party issues. The House Minority Leader has a similar position to that of the Minority Leader in the Senate.

INAUGURATION

Presidential elections take place in November, with the new President sworn into office on the following 20 January*. Here's a guide to Inauguration Day.

1 The incoming President and First Lady attend a church service, a tradition that began with Franklin Roosevelt in 1933.

2 The incoming President and First Lady are then (usually) hosted by their departing counterparts at the White House before heading to the Capitol.

3 On a specially constructed platform on the Capitol's West Front, the Vice President takes the oath first, followed by the President (administered usually by the Chief Justice of the Supreme Court; in the case of the Vice President another official usually does the honours). The right hand is raised and the left hand is place on a Bible for the oath.

4 The President officially takes office at 12.01pm.

5 The President delivers the Inaugural Address, setting the tone for their time in office. Poets and musicians selected by the new President add to the occasion.

6 After lunch, the President and the First Family proceed to the White House at the head of a parade, usually stopping their motorcade at some point to make some of the journey on foot and to shake hands with campaign supporters and other wellwishers.

7 Celebrations continue long into the evening, with the President and First Lady attending several balls.

* Should 20 January be a Sunday, the President takes the oath in a smaller ceremony, with a public inauguration taking place the following day.
Note: Until 1933, the inauguration was held in March but, because a four-month period with an outgoing President in charge was deemed to be a time of inaction, the Constitution was amended to bring forward the ceremony.

MIDTERMS

Elections held roughly halfway through a President's term of office are known as midterms. Every seat in the House of Representatives and around one-third of seats in the Senate are contested and so these elections provide a snapshot of the President's popularity. Also, the outcome may strengthen or weaken the President's ability to govern if control of Congress changes.

THE SHORTEST PRESIDENTIAL TERMS

The longest period in office served by a US President was that of Franklin Roosevelt – 12 years 39 days. Many other Presidents served eight years (or close to it), as a result of two election wins, but a number failed to even make it to the standard first-term limit of four years, either because they died or because they inherited the Presidency from their deceased or resigned predecessor part of the way through a term. Here are the shortest-serving Presidents (not including the most recently elected incumbent, Joe Biden).

	President	Term
1	Franklin Roosevelt	12 years 39 days
35	John Tyler	3 years 334 days
36	Andrew Johnson	3 years 323 days
37	Chester Arthur	3 years 166 days
38	John F Kennedy	2 years 306 days
39	Millard Fillmore	2 years 238 days
40	Gerald Ford	2 years 164 days
41	Warren Harding	2 years 151 days
42	Zachary Taylor	1 year 127 days
43	James Garfield	199 days
44	William Harrison	31 days

PRESIDENTS DEPICTED ON MOUNT RUSHMORE

Washington · Jefferson · Lincoln · Theodore Roosevelt

SECOND NAMES OF SOME US FIRST LADIES

Jane *Means* Pierce
Lucy *Ware* Hayes
Edith *Kermit* Roosevelt
Ellen *Louise* Wilson
Florence *Mabel* Harding
Grace *Anna* Coolidge
Anna Eleanor Roosevelt
Bess *Virginia* Truman
Mamie *Geneva* Eisenhower

Jacqueline *Lee* Kennedy
Claudia *Alta* Johnson
Thelma *Catherine* Nixon
Betty *Anne* Ford
Eleanor Rosalynn Carter
Hillary *Diane* Clinton
Laura *Lane* Bush
Michelle *LaVaughan* Obama
Jill *Tracy* Biden

POLITICS IN EUROPE

THE EUROPEAN UNION

The foundations of the European Union (EU) lie in the European Coal and Steel Community, an association of six countries formed in 1952. The six countries went on to create the European Economic Community (EEC) through the Treaty of Rome in 1957, which came into effect in 1958. Closer ties between member countries continued to be forged with the development of the EEC into the European Union in 1993. There are currently 27 member states and their years of accession are outlined below.

Year Joined	Country/ies
1958	Belgium, France, Germany, Italy, Luxembourg, Netherlands
1973	Denmark, Ireland
1981	Greece
1986	Portugal, Spain
1995	Austria, Finland, Sweden
2004	Cyprus, Czech Republic, Estonia, Hungary, Latvia, Lithuania, Malta, Poland, Slovakia, Slovenia
2007	Bulgaria, Romania
2013	Croatia

Note: The UK became a member in 1973 but left in 2020.

THE OLDEST PARLIAMENT

The oldest parliament in the world is considered to be Iceland's Althing or Alþingi, originally housed in Thingvellir and now in Reykjavik. This was suspended from 1800 to 1845 but has been active otherwise since c.930.

THE PRESIDENTS OF EUROPE

Presidents of
the European Parliament
1958 ....Robert Schuman *FR*
1960 ....Hans Furler *WG*
1962 ....Gaetano Martino *IT*
1964 .... Jean Duvieusart *BE*
1965 ....Victor Leemans *BE*
1966 ....Alain Poher *FR*
1969 .... Mario Scelba *IT*
1971 ....Walter Behrendt *WG*
1973 ....Cornelis Berkhouwer *NL*
1975 ....Georges Spénale *FR*
1977 ....Emilio Colombo *IT*
1979 .... Simone Veil *FR*
1982 ....Piet Dankert *NL*
1984 ....Pierre Pflimlin *FR*
1987 ....Henry Plumb *UK*
1989 ....Enrique Barón Crespo *ES*
1992 ....Egon Klepsch *DE*
1994 ....Klaus Hänsch *DE*
1997 ....José María Gil-Robles *ES*
1999 ....Nicole Fontaine *FR*
2002 ....Pat Cox *IE*
2004 ....Josep Borrell Fontelles *ES*
2007 .... Hans-Gert Pöttering *DE*
2009 .... Jerzy Buzek *PL*
2012 ....Martin Schulz *DE*

2017 ....Antonio Tajani *IT*
2019 ....David Sassoli *IT*
2022 ....Roberta Metsola *MT*

Presidents of
the European Council*
2009 ....Herman Van Rompuy *BE*
2014 .... Donald Tusk *PL*
2019 ....Charles Michel *BE*

Presidents of
the European Commission
1958 ....Walter Hallstein *DE*
1967 .... Jean Rey *BE*
1970 .... Franco Maria Malfatti *IT*
1972 .... Sicco Mansholt *NL*
1973 ....François-Xavier Ortoli *FR*
1977 ....Roy Jenkins *UK*
1981 .... Gaston Thorn *LU*
1985 ....Jacques Delors *FR*
1995 ....Jacques Santer *LU*
1999 .... Manuel Marin† *ES*
1999 .... Romano Prodi *IT*
2004 ....José Manuel Barroso *PT*
2014 ....Jean-Claude Juncker *LU*
2019 .... Ursula von der Leyen *DE*

* Before 2010, the role of President of the European Council rotated around the various national leaders every six months.
† Acting President.

OFFICIAL LANGUAGES OF THE EUROPEAN UNION

Bulgarian · Croatian · Czech · Danish · Dutch · English · Estonian
Finnish · French · German · Greek · Hungarian · Irish · Italian · Latvian
Lithuanian · Maltese · Polish · Portuguese · Romanian · Slovak
Slovenian · Spanish · Swedish

NEW POST-WAR EUROPEAN REPUBLICS

Kingdoms or dominions that became republics after the Second World War.

1946 .... Albania, Bulgaria, Hungary, Italy, Yugoslavia	1949 .... Ireland
1947 .... Romania	1960 .... Cyprus
	1974 .... Greece, Malta

PRESIDENTS OF FRANCE

France declared itself a republic in 1792 after the French Revolution, with power transferred from the Monarchy to a governing body known as the National Convention. The President of the National Convention, while arguably the head of state, served for only a two-week term so numerous figures took on the role. The National Convention was replaced by the five-man Directory with collective leadership, before that was replaced by the Consulate, with Napoleon Bonaparte as the First Consul, later to be elected Emperor. The first recognisable President of France was Louis-Napoléon Bonaparte in 1848 but he soon declared himself Emperor. Second World War occupation by Germany meant no Presidents 1940–47.

Second Republic (1848–52)
1848 ..... Louis-Napoléon Bonaparte

Third Republic (1870–1940)
1871 .... Adolphe Thiers
1873 .... Patrice de MacMahon
1879 .... Jules Grévy
1887 .... Sadi Carnot
1894 .... Jean Casimir-Périer
1895 .... Félix Faure
1899 .... Émile Loubet
1906 .... Armand Fallières
1913 .... Raymond Poincaré
1920 .... Paul Deschanel
1920 .... Alexandre Millerand
1924 .... Gaston Doumergue
1931 .... Paul Doumer

1932 .... Albert Lebrun

Fourth Republic (1946–58)
1947 .... Vincent Auriol
1954 .... René Coty

Fifth Republic (1958–)
1959 .... Charles de Gaulle
1969 .... Alain Poher*
1969 .... Georges Pompidou
1974 .... Alain Poher*
1974 .... Valéry Giscard d'Estaing
1981 .... François Mitterrand
1995 .... Jacques Chirac
2007 .... Nicolas Sarkozy
2012 .... François Hollande
2017 .... Emmanuel Macron

* Acting President.

ANOTHER GOVERNMENT, PER FAVORE

Governments in Italy are notoriously unstable. Since the country became a republic in 1946, there have been no fewer than 68 different administrations.

OFFICIAL RESIDENCES IN EUROPE

Country	Office	Residence
Austria	President	Hofburg, Vienna
	Chancellor	Ballhausplatz 2, Vienna
Belgium	Prime Minister	rue de la Loi 16, Brussels
Denmark	Prime Minister	Marienborg, near Copenhagen
Finland	President	Presidentinlinna, Helsinki
	Prime Minister	Kesäranta, Helsinki
France	President	Palais de l'Elysée, Paris
	Prime Minister	Hôtel de Matignon, Paris
Germany	President	Schloss Bellevue, Berlin
	Chancellor	Bundeskanzleramt, Berlin
Greece	Prime Minister	Mégaro Maxímou, Athens
Hungary	President	Sándor-palota, Budapest
Iceland	President	Bessastaðir, Álftanes
Ireland	President	Áras an Uachtaráin, Dublin
Italy	President	Palazzo del Quirinale, Rome
	Prime Minister	Palazzo Chigi, Rome
Netherlands	Prime Minister	Catshuis, The Hague
Norway	Prime Minister	Inkognitogata 18, Oslo
Poland	President	Pałac Prezydencki, Warsaw
Portugal	President	Palácio de Belém, Lisbon
	Prime Minister	Palacete de São Bento, Lisbon
Romania	President	Palatul Cotroceni, Bucharest
Spain	Prime Minister	Palacio de la Moncloa, Madrid
Sweden	Prime Minister	Sagerska palatset, Stockholm
Ukraine	President	Mariinskyi palats, Kyiv

THE YOUNGEST PRESIDENT

When Emmanuel Macron was elected in 2017 at the age of 39, he became the youngest ever President of France, assuming this status from the first President, Louis-Napoléon Bonaparte, who was 40 when voted in, in 1848.

THE MAIN EUROPEAN UNION INSTITUTIONS

The European Parliament
The body that makes the laws of the EU. Its 705 Members (MEPs) are directly elected by the citizens of EU countries every five years (before 1979, Members were nominated by the national parliaments). The Parliament also scrutinises the work of other EU bodies and, along with the European Council, sets the EU's budget. The President of the European Parliament is elected by MEPs for a term of two-and-a-half years. The official seat of the European Parliament is in Strasbourg (in a modern, glassy, oval building named after the pioneering French MEP Louise Weiss) but it has also bases in Brussels (where committees meet) and Luxembourg (home of the administrative staff).

The European Council
Comprised of the heads of state of EU member countries, this body sets out the direction and priorities of the EU's work. It meets four times a year. The President of the European Council is elected by the members of the Council for a two-and-a-half-year term. The administrative centre is the modern, cube-shaped Europa building in Brussels.

The European Commission
The executive wing of the EU, with membership comprised of one commissioner appointed by each member country. It proposes new laws, prepares budgets, monitors expenditure and negotiates new international agreements on behalf of the EU. The President of the European Commission is nominated by the European Council and needs a majority of votes in the European Parliament to gain election for a five-year term. The headquarters of the European Commission is the Berlaymont in Brussels – the cross-shaped 1960s structure built on the site of the former Berlaymont convent – but there are also departments in Luxembourg, as well as offices in all EU countries.

The Council of the European Union
An assembly of Government ministers from all EU member countries, with representation varying according to the subject under discussion. The office of the President rotates among the countries twice a year. The body plays a major role in negotiating and approving EU legislation and co-ordinates the various policies of member countries in areas such as economics, education and culture. It also adopts the EU budget, approves and concludes international negotiations and agreements, and sets out the EU's shared foreign and security policies in liaison with the European Council.

OTHER KEY EUROPEAN UNION INSTITUTIONS

The Court of Justice of the European Union

The Court of Justice of the European Union (CJEU) actually consists of two separate courts. The first, known simply as the Court of Justice, arbitrates on how EU law is interpreted and ensures all member countries abide by their legal obligations. All countries nominate one judge, who serves for a six-year term. The second court is the General Court, which deals with actions against the EU and its institutions by member states or individuals, with countries each providing two judges. Both courts are based in Luxembourg.

The Court of Auditors

Comprised of one member per country, each serving a six-year term, the Court of Auditors is the body that scrutinises the budgets of EU institutions and aims to improve financial management. It is based in Luxembourg.

The European Central Bank

Established in 1998 and based in Frankfurt, this is the central bank for the Eurozone. It sets monetary policy for the countries that have adopted the euro, seeks to maintain financial stability, controls inflation and supervises banks operating within the area.

THE FIRST WOMEN PRESIDENTS IN EUROPE

Country	President	Year
Croatia	Kolinda Grabar-Kitarović	2015
East Germany	Sabine Bergmann-Pohl	1990
Estonia	Kersti Kaljulaid	2016
Finland	Tarja Halonen	2000
Georgia	Salome Zourabichvili	2018
Greece	Katerina Sakellaropoulou	2020
Hungary	Katalin Novák	2022
Iceland	Vigdís Finnbogadóttir	1980
Ireland	Mary Robinson	1990
Kosovo	Atifete Jahjaga	2011
Latvia	Vaira Vīķe-Freiberga	1999
Lithuania	Dalia Grybauskaitė	2009
Malta	Agatha Barbara	1982
Moldova	Maia Sandu	2020
Slovakia	Zuzana Čaputová	2019
Switzerland	Ruth Dreifuss	1999

EFTA

The European Free Trade Association (EFTA) was founded in 1960 to promote free trade and economic integration among countries that did not wish to join the European Economic Community (EEC). Initially, there were seven members – Austria, Denmark, Norway, Portugal, Sweden, Switzerland and the United Kingdom; today there are four. These countries – with the exception of Switzerland, which declined to join – enjoy access to the free market of the EU as part of the European Economic Area (EEA).

Iceland · Liechtenstein · Norway · Switzerland

LEADERS OF IRELAND

Presidents

1938	Douglas Hyde
1945	Sean T O'Ceallaigh
1959	Eamon de Valera
1973	Erskine Childers
1974	Cearbhail Ó Dálaigh
1976	Patrick J Hillery
1990	Mary Robinson
1997	Mary McAleese
2011	Michael D Higgins

Taoisigh*

1922	William T Cosgrave
1932	Eamon de Valera
1948	John Costello
1951	Eamon de Valera
1954	John Costello
1957	Eamon de Valera
1959	Sean Lemass
1966	Jack Lynch
1973	Liam Cosgrave
1977	Jack Lynch
1979	Charles Haughey
1981	Garret FitzGerald
1982	Charles Haughey
1982	Garret FitzGerald
1987	Charles Haughey
1992	Albert Reynolds
1994	John Bruton
1997	Bertie Ahern
2008	Brian Cowen
2011	Enda Kenny
2017	Leo Varadkar
2020	Micheál Martin

* Plural of Taoiseach (Prime Minister).

Note: The head of state of Ireland and guardian of the Constitution is the President, who is elected by citizens for a term of seven years. The head of the Government is the Taoiseach, a title that has been in effect since 1937. Government leaders before this time – during the existence of the Irish Free State, 1922–37 – were known by the title President of the Executive Council.

SEATS IN THE EUROPEAN PARLIAMENT

Including the President, there are 705 Members of the European Parliament (MEPs). The number of seats allocated to each country is broadly in line with its population, although no country can have fewer than six seats or more than 96. Following the UK's departure from the European Union in 2020, the seat allocation was amended and the numbers below were applied.

Germany 96	Greece 21	Ireland 13
France.......................79	Hungary....................21	Croatia 12
Italy...........................76	Portugal....................21	Lithuania..................11
Spain..........................59	Sweden 21	Latvia...........................8
Poland 52	Austria......................19	Slovenia.......................8
Romania....................33	Bulgaria....................17	Estonia 7
Netherlands 29	Denmark...................14	Cyprus.........................6
Belgium.....................21	Slovakia....................14	Luxembourg..............6
Czech Republic.......21	Finland.....................14	Malta 6

Note: At the time of leaving the EU, the UK had 73 seats.

THE REICHSTAG

The Reichstag building in Berlin is the meeting place of the Bundestag, or the lower house of the country's parliament, and is one of the most poignant symbols of German democracy.

The building was constructed in the late 19th century, to designs by the German architect Paul Wallot, and became home of the Reichstag – as the lower house was known at the time – in 1894.

It resumed that role after the First World War until it was destroyed by fire in 1933 – a landmark event that allowed the Chancellor, Adolf Hitler, to accuse his political opponents of arson and seize dictatorial powers.

Partial reconstruction repaired damage sustained during the Second World War but then a major restoration, led by the British architect Norman Foster, followed the reunification of Germany in 1990.

The building became the permanent home of the Bundestag in 1999, when the seat of the German Government was moved back to Berlin after its temporary post-war residence in Bonn.

THE SOVIET UNION

Once the world's largest country, the Soviet Union or USSR (Union of Soviet Socialist Republics) was created in 1922 after the Russian Revolution. When the USSR eventually collapsed in 1991, there were 15 constituent territories.

Armenia · Azerbaijan · Belarus · Estonia · Georgia · Kazakhstan
Kyrgyzstan · Latvia · Lithuania · Moldova · Russia · Tajikistan
Turkmenistan · Ukraine · Uzbekistan

THE WARSAW PACT

Established in 1955, the Warsaw Treaty of Friendship, Cooperation and Mutual Assistance, or the Warsaw Pact, was central and eastern Europe's answer to NATO, although it also served as a means of reinforcing the influence of the Soviet Union over its satellite countries. The Pact remained in force until the democratisation of former communist countries in 1989 and was formally wound up in 1991. The member countries were as follows.

Albania* · Bulgaria · Czechoslovakia · East Germany† · Hungary
Poland · Romania · Soviet Union

* Left in 1968. † Left in 1990.

THE ELYSÉE PALACE (PALAIS DE L'ELYSÉE)

The Elysée Palace in Paris began life as a nobleman's house in the early 1700s. Later residents included Madame de Pompadour – mistress of King Louis XV – and Napoléon Bonaparte, who lived there as Emperor in his final years in power.

The first President to take up residence was Louis Napoléon, in 1848, although he moved out when assuming the title of Emperor Napoléon III four years later.

With the establishment of the Third Republic in 1874, the property resumed its role as the President's official residence, an arrangement that continued until it was vacated during the Second World War.

With the election of Charles de Gaulle in 1958, the Elysée again became the President's residence and also the place where French Government ministers meet on a weekly basis.

THE FIRST WOMEN PRIME MINISTERS IN EUROPE

Country	Prime Minister	Year
Austria	Brigitte Bierlein*	2019
Belgium	Sophie Wilmès	2019
Croatia	Jadranka Kosor	2009
Denmark	Helle Thorning-Schmidt	2011
Estonia	Kaja Kallas	2021
Finland	Anneli Jäätteenmäki	2003
France	Edith Cresson	1991
Germany	Angela Merkel*	2005
Iceland	Jóhanna Sigurðardóttir	2009
Latvia	Laimdota Straujuma	2014
Lithuania	Kazimira Prunskienė	1990
Moldova	Zinaida Greceanîi	2008
Norway	Gro Harlem Brundtland	1981
Poland	Hanna Suchocka	1992
Portugal	Maria de Lourdes Pintasilgo	1979
Romania	Viorica Dăncilă	2018
Serbia	Ana Brnabić	2017
Slovakia	Iveta Radičová	2010
Slovenia	Alenka Bratušek	2013
Sweden	Magdalena Andersson	2021
Turkey	Tansu Çiller	1993
Ukraine	Yulia Tymoshenko	2005
UK	Margaret Thatcher	1979
Yugoslavia	Milka Planinc	1982

* Officially known as Chancellor.

BENELUX

Taking its name from the initial letters of its member countries, Benelux is an economic and political union established by Belgium, the Netherlands and Luxembourg. The union was forged in 1948 to step up financial and trade co-operation, establishing tariff-free movement of goods and services and an open labour market, a process that was formalised in the 1958 Treaty of the Benelux Economic Union. Through the various institutions it set up, Benelux provided a template for the future European Economic Community and the European Union, of which the three countries are also members.

LEADERS OF THE SOVIET UNION

The de facto leader of the Soviet Union was the man who held the position of Chairman (at times known as First Secretary) of the Communist Party.

1922 .... Vladimir Ilich Lenin	1964 .... Leonid Brezhnev
1924 .... Joseph Stalin	1982 .... Yury Andropov
1953 .... Georgy Malenkov	1984 .... Konstantin Chernenko
1953 .... Nikita Khrushchev	1985 .... Mikhail Gorbachev

PRESIDENTS OF RUSSIA

The Presidents of Russia following the collapse of the Soviet Union in 1991.

1991 .... Boris Yeltsin	2008 .... Dmitry Medvedev
2000 .... Vladimir Putin	2012 .... Vladimir Putin

A SHORTER PRESIDENCY

In 2000, voters in France decided, through a referendum, to shorten the term of office served by the country's President. Since 1873, the term had been set at seven years but this was now swept aside and replaced by a five-year period. This move helped to 'modernise' French politics, according to some advocates, making the office of the Presidency more responsive to political change. It also helped to minimise political conflicts that arose from the fact that the National Assembly – already elected for five-year terms – was often out of kilter with the Presidency, leading to difficult periods of 'co-habitation' between the President and a Government of a different political persuasion. The new term limit came into force in 2002.

NICKNAMES OF EUROPEAN POLITICIANS

Bulldozer............ Jacques Chirac *FR*	Pear .... Helmut Kohl *DE*
Constable ...... Charles de Gaulle *FR*	President Bling-Bling........................
Flanby........... François Hollande *FR*	Nicolas Sarkozy *FR*
Jupiter......... Emmanuel Macron *FR*	Rosie .... Ursula von der Layen *DE*
Knight .... Silvio Berlusconi *IT*	Sphinx ....François Mitterand *FR*
Mutti.................. Angela Merkel *DE*	Viktator............... Viktor Orban *HU*

THE KREMLIN

Now a byword for the Russian Government, the Kremlin – 'citadel' in Russian – in central Moscow is a collection of architecturally exceptional palaces, churches and towers, tucked away behind distinctive red-brick, crenellated walls that date from the 15th century.

Once the home of the tsars, the structure regained its political importance following the Russian Revolution, when the seat of power moved back here from St Petersburg and the Great Kremlin Palace, within the fortress, hosted sessions of the Supreme Soviet (the legislative assembly of the USSR).

Today, the Kremlin is home to the official residence of the President of Russia. Adjacent is Red Square where the embalmed body of the father of the Revolution, Vladimir Lenin, lies on public display in a mausoleum located next to the Kremlin wall.

THE EUROZONE

So far 19 countries (listed below) have adopted the euro as their currency since it was launched in 2002. A number of other EU countries are waiting for the necessary economic conditions to be met before joining this group.

Austria · Belgium · Cyprus · Estonia · Finland · France · Germany · Greece
Ireland · Italy · Latvia · Lithuania · Luxembourg · Malta · Netherlands
Portugal · Slovakia · Slovenia · Spain

Note: Some other countries use the euro as a result of agreements with the EU, most notably Andorra, Monaco, San Marino and Vatican City. Also, Kosovo and Montenegro use the euro as a de facto currency, despite not having agreements with the EU, in the same way that other countries use the US dollar.

IRISH PARTY NAMES IN TRANSLATION

Party	Meaning of Name
Aontú	Unity/Agreement
Fianna Fáil	Soldiers of Destiny/Warriors of Ireland
Fine Gael	Tribe of the Gaels/Gaelic Nation
Sinn Féin	Ourselves Alone

MAJOR POLITICAL PARTIES OF FRANCE

Left	Centre	Right
EE Les Verts*	En Marche	Agir
La France Insoumise	Horizons	Debout la France
Parti Communiste	Mouvement Démocrate	Rassemblement National
Parti Radical de Gauche	UDI†	Les Républicains
Parti Socialiste		

* Europe Ecologie Les Verts. † Union des Démocrates et Indépendants.

CHANCELLORS OF GERMANY

In Germany, while the President is officially the head of state, political leadership is provided by the Chancellor as the head of the Government.

German Empire (1871–1918)
1871	Otto von Bismarck
1890	Leo von Caprivi
1894	Chlodwig Karl Viktor*
1900	Bernhard von Bülow
1909	Theobald von Bethmann Hollweg
1917	Georg Michaelis
1917	Georg von Hertling
1918	Max von Baden
1918	Friedrich Ebert

Weimar Republic (1919–33)
1919	Philipp Scheidemann
1919	Gustav Bauer
1920	Hermann Müller
1920	Konstantin Fehrenbach
1921	Joseph Wirth
1922	Wilhelm Cuno
1923	Gustav Stresemann
1923	Wilhelm Marx
1925	Hans Luther

1926	Wilhelm Marx
1928	Hermann Müller
1930	Heinrich Brüning
1932	Franz von Papen
1932	Kurt von Schleicher

Third Reich (1933–45)
1933	Adolf Hitler
1945	Joseph Goebbels

Federal Republic of Germany (1949–)
1949	Konrad Adenauer
1963	Ludwig Erhard
1966	Kurt Georg Kiesinger
1969	Willy Brandt
1974	Helmut Schmidt
1982	Helmut Kohl
1998	Gerhard Schröder
2005	Angela Merkel
2021	Olaf Scholz

* Prince of Hohenlohe-Schillingsfürst.

POLITICS IN
THE WIDER WORLD

THE UNITED NATIONS

The United Nations was founded in 1945 to replace the League of Nations (in operation since 1919). Describing itself as 'one place where the world's nations can gather together, discuss common problems and find shared solutions,' its motto today is 'Peace, dignity and equality on a healthy planet'.

FOUNDER MEMBERS OF THE UNITED NATIONS

Argentina, Australia, Belorussia (now Belarus), Belgium, Bolivia, Brazil, Canada, Chile, China, Colombia, Costa Rica, Cuba, Czechoslovakia*, Denmark, Dominican Republic, Ecuador, Egypt, El Salvador, Ethiopia, France, Greece, Guatemala, Haiti, Honduras, India, Iran, Iraq, Lebanon, Liberia, Luxembourg, Mexico, Netherlands, New Zealand, Nicaragua, Norway, Panama, Paraguay, Peru, Philippines, Poland, Saudi Arabia, South Africa, Syria, Turkey, Ukraine, UK, United States, Uruguay, USSR (now Russia), Venezuela, Yugoslavia*

Note: Countries that joined the UN at its inception in 1945.
* Country no longer exists: former territories later joined the UN under new country names.

133

UNITED NATIONS MEMBER COUNTRIES

Year Joined	Country/ies
1945	See *Founder Members* (p. 133)
1946	Afghanistan, Iceland, Sweden, Thailand
1947	Pakistan, Yemen
1948	Myanmar
1949	Israel
1950	Indonesia
1955	Albania, Austria, Bulgaria, Cambodia, Finland, Hungary, Ireland, Italy, Jordan, Laos, Libya, Nepal, Portugal, Romania, Spain, Sri Lanka
1956	Japan, Morocco, Sudan, Tunisia
1957	Ghana, Malaysia
1958	Guinea
1960	Benin, Burkina Faso, Cameroon, Cent. African Rep., Chad, Rep. of Congo, DR Congo, Côte d'Ivoire, Cyprus, Gabon, Madagascar, Mali, Niger, Nigeria, Senegal, Somalia, Togo
1961	Mauritania, Mongolia, Sierra Leone, Tanzania
1962	Algeria, Burundi, Jamaica, Rwanda, Trinidad and Tobago, Uganda
1963	Kenya, Kuwait
1964	Malawi, Malta, Zambia
1965	The Gambia, Maldives, Singapore
1966	Barbados, Botswana, Guyana, Lesotho
1968	Equatorial Guinea, Eswatini, Mauritius
1970	Fiji
1971	Bahrain, Bhutan, Oman, Qatar, United Arab Emirates
1973	The Bahamas
1974	Bangladesh, Grenada, Guinea-Bissau
1975	Cabo Verde, Comoros, Mozambique, Papua N Guinea, São Tome and Principe, Suriname
1976	Angola, Samoa, Seychelles,
1977	Djibouti, Vietnam
1978	Dominica, Solomon Islands
1979	St Lucia
1980	St Vincent and the Grenadines, Zimbabwe
1981	Antigua and Barbuda, Belize, Vanuatu
1983	St Kitts and Nevis
1984	Brunei
1990	Germany, Liechtenstein, Namibia
1991	Estonia, Latvia, Lithuania, Marshall Islands, Micronesia, North Korea, South Korea
1992	Armenia, Azerbaijan, Bosnia and Herzegovina, Croatia, Georgia, Kazakhstan, Kyrgyzstan, Moldova, San Marino, Slovenia, Tajikistan, Turkmenistan, Uzbekistan
1993	Andorra, Czech Rep., Eritrea, Monaco, North Macedonia, Slovakia
1994	Palau
1999	Kiribati, Nauru, Tonga
2000	Tuvalu
2002	East Timor, Switzerland
2006	Montenegro, Serbia
2011	South Sudan

THE COUNTRY WITH THREE CAPITALS

The Government of South Africa is based across three cities. Cape Town is where the parliament sits and is therefore known as the legislative capital, the Supreme Court convenes in Bloemfontein, making it the judicial capital, and Pretoria is known as the administrative capital as this is where the Cabinet meets. Pretoria is also the location of Mahlamba Ndlopfu ('New Dawn', known as Libertas until 1995), the official residence of the President.

LEADERS OF CHINA

Leadership since the proclamation of the People's Republic of China in 1949.

Communist Party Leaders*

1949	Mao Zedong	1989	Jiang Zemin
1976	Hua Guofeng	2002	Hu Jintao
1981	Hu Yaobang	2012	Xi Jinping
1987	Zhao Ziyang		

Premiers†

1949	Zhou Enlai	1998	Zhu Rongji
1976	Hua Guofeng	2003	Wen Jiabao
1980	Zhao Ziyang	2013	Li Keqiang
1987	Li Peng		

* The official title until 1982 was Chairman; since that time the official title has been General Secretary. † Often referred to as Prime Minister.

A BUZZING PLACE TO WORK

New Zealand's legislature meets in Parliament House, an early 20th-century building in Wellington. Since 1977, this has been flanked by a modern executive building where the Cabinet meets and the Prime Minister and other members of the Government have their offices. Commonly known as the 'Beehive', because of its distinctive skep-like shape, the ten-story structure took ten years to complete and is based on initial designs by the British architect Basil Spence. Two other buildings complete Wellington's Parliamentary campus – the Parliamentary Library and the 22-storey Bowen House, which houses the offices of some MPs and committee rooms.

BRICS

Founded as BRIC, a name derived from the initials of its members, in 2006, this association of four nations with emerging economies expanded with the addition of South Africa in 2010, when the name evolved into BRICS. Member nations represent more than 40 per cent of the world's population.

Brazil · Russia · India · China · South Africa

THE MAIN INSTITUTIONS OF THE UNITED NATIONS

General Assembly

The major body for decision making, with all UN member countries represented. The General Assembly meets annually, with many heads of state or heads of government in attendance. It deals with issues of security, peace, budgets and possible new members.

Security Council

The body that leads the way in matters of security and aggression, determining where it is appropriate for countries to engage in peace talks, acting to impose sanctions on aggressive countries and even, in extremis, approving military action.

Economic and Social Council

Economic, social, cultural and environmental issues are the brief of this body, which designs policies, sets out recommendations and implements agreed goals.

International Court of Justice

A court that arbitrates on international disputes and provides legal advice to other UN bodies. The only major UN body not operating from New York, the ICJ is based in the Peace Palace in The Hague, Netherlands. There are 15 judges, each elected on nine-year terms, with no more than one judge allowed per country.

Secretariat

This is the administrative and operational wing of the UN, headed by the Secretary-General. The Secretariat co-ordinates activities, prepares agendas and briefing papers, and executes decisions taken by other arms of the organisation.

Trusteeship Council

Largely defunct since the mid-1990s, this body was set up to monitor the administration of various 'Trust Territories' – countries/regions that were under the supervision of other countries while they were prepared for self-governance or possibly full independence.

A TIMELINE OF WOMEN'S SUFFRAGE

The years in which women were given the vote in some selected countries.

1893 .... New Zealand
1902 .... Australia
1906 .... Finland
1907 .... Norway
1915 .... Denmark, Iceland
1917 .... Canada, Russia
1918 .... Austria, Czechoslovakia, Estonia, Germany, Hungary, Latvia, Lithuania, Poland, UK
1919 .... Belgium, Luxembourg, Netherlands, Sweden
1920 .... Albania, USA
1922 .... Ireland
1929 .... Ecuador, Puerto Rico
1930 .... South Africa, Turkey
1931 .... Spain, Sri Lanka
1932 .... Brazil, Thailand, Uruguay
1933 .... Portugal
1934 .... Cuba
1935 .... India, Myanmar
1937 .... Philippines
1939 .... El Salvador
1941 .... Indonesia
1942 .... Dominican Republic
1944 .... Bermuda, France, Jamaica
1945 .... Bulgaria, Italy, Japan, Trinidad and Tobago
1946 .... Liberia, Portugal, Romania, Venezuela, Vietnam
1947 .... Argentina, Bangladesh, Malta, Pakistan

1948 .... Israel, South Korea
1949 .... Chile, China, Syria
1950 .... Barbados, Haiti
1951 .... Antigua, Dominica, Grenada, Tonga
1952 .... Bolivia, Greece, Lebanon
1953 .... Mexico
1954 .... Colombia
1955 ... Cambodia, Ethiopia, Ghana, Honduras, Nicaragua, Peru
1956 .... Egypt, Gabon, Madagascar, Mali, Niger
1958 .... Laos, Mauritius
1960 .... Cyprus, San Marino
1961 .... Paraguay, Rwanda
1962 ...... Algeria, Bahamas, Monaco
1963 .... Iran, Kenya
1964 .... Afghanistan, Libya, Malawi, Papua New Guinea, Sudan
1965 .... Botswana
1966 .... Lesotho
1967 .... DR Congo, Yemen
1968 .... Nauru, Eswatini
1971 .... Switzerland
1974 .... Jordan
1975 ....Angola, Cape Verde, Mozambique
1984 .... Liechtenstein
1002 .... Bahrain
2005 .... Kuwait
2011 .... Saudi Arabia

Note: Some regions/states of the above countries granted suffrage earlier than the date declared for the whole country. Restrictions to women's suffrage – based on issues such as age, colour, education and wealth – applied in a number of countries for some time afterwards. In some countries, the franchise was suspended when oppressive regimes took over.

THE FIRST WOMEN PRESIDENTS OUTSIDE EUROPE

Country	President	Year
Argentina	Isabel Perón*	1974
Barbados	Sandra Mason	2021
Brazil	Dilma Rousseff	2011
Chile	Michelle Bachelet	2006
Costa Rica	Laura Chinchilla	2010
Ethiopia	Sahle-Work Zewde	2018
Guyana	Janet Jagan	1997
Honduras	Xiomara Castro	2022
India	Pratibha Patil	2007
Indonesia	Megawati Sukarnoputri	2001
Liberia	Ellen Johnson Sirleaf	2006
Kyrgyzstan	Roza Otunbayeva	2010
Malawi	Joyce Banda	2012
Marshall Islands	Hilda Heine	2016
Mauritius	Ameenah Gurib-Fakim	2015
Nepal	Bidya Devi Bhandari	2015
Nicaragua	Violeta Chamorro	1990
Panama	Mireya Moscoso	1999
Philippines	Corazon Aquino	1986
Singapore	Halimah Yacob	2017
South Korea	Park Geun-Hye	2013
Sri Lanka	Chandrika Kumaratunga	1994
Taiwan	Tsai Ing-wen	2016
Tanzania	Samia Suluhu Hassan	2021
Trinidad and Tobago	Paula-Mae Weekes	2018

* Unelected: the first elected women President was Cristina Fernández de Kirchner in 2007.

THE FIVE EYES

Founded in the wake of the Second World War, the Five Eyes (FVEY) is an intelligence partnership between the following five countries who share confidential information. The name is derived from the classification applied to secret documents and the 'eyes' that are permitted to see them.

Australia · Canada · New Zealand · UK · USA

THE AFRICAN UNION

The African Union (AU) was officially established in 2002 as a replacement for the Organisation for African Unity (OAU) that had existed from 1963 to 1999 to rid the continent of the last traces of colonialism, foster liaison and solidarity between countries, defend the sovereignty of member states and promote international co-operation. The decision to remodel the OAU into the AU was inspired by the need for less emphasis on colonial issues and more on the economic and democratic development of the continent.

Year Joined*	Country/ies
1963	Algeria, Benin, Burkina Faso, Burundi, Cameroon, Central African Republic, Chad, Rep. of Congo, DR Congo, Côte d'Ivoire, Egypt, Ethiopia, Gabon, Ghana, Guinea, Kenya, Liberia, Libya, Madagascar, Mali, Mauritania, Morocco†, Niger, Nigeria, Rwanda, Senegal, Sierra Leone, Somalia, Sudan, Tanzania, Togo, Tunisia, Uganda
1964	Malawi, Zambia
1965	Gambia
1966	Botswana, Lesotho
1968	Equatorial Guinea, Eswatini, Mauritius
1973	Guinea-Bissau
1975	Angola, Cabo Verde, Comoros, Mozambique, São Tomé and Príncipe
1976	Seychelles
1977	Djibouti
1980	Zimbabwe
1982	Sahrawi Republic
1990	Namibia
1993	Eritrea
1994	South Africa
2011	South Sudan

* Either the OAU or AU. † Left in 1984, rejoined in 2017.

THE SECURITY COUNCIL OF THE UNITED NATIONS

Membership of the UN Security Council is limited to 15 countries. Five of these are permanent members with the other ten elected to sit on the Council for a two-year term. The five permanent members are:

China* · France · Russia† · UK · USA

* The Republic of China (Taiwan) until 1971 when replaced by the People's Republic of China. † Soviet Union until 1991.

UNITED NATIONS FUNDS, PROGRAMMES AND AGENCIES

Entity	Full Title	HQ
FAO	Food and Agriculture Organization	Rome
ICAO	International Civil Aviation Organization	Montreal
IFAD	International Fund for Agricultural Development	Rome
ILO	International Labor Organization	Geneva
IMF	International Monetary Fund	Washington, DC
IMO	International Maritime Organization	London
ITU	International Telecommunication Union	Geneva
UN Women	United Nations Entity for Gender Equality and the Empowerment of Women	New York
UN-HABITAT	United Nations Human Settlements Programme	Nairobi
UNAIDS	Joint United Nations Programme on HIV/AIDS	Geneva
UNDP	United Nationals Development Programme	New York
UNEP	United Nations Environment Programme	Nairobi
UNESCO	United Nations Educational, Scientific and Cultural Organization	Paris
UNFPA	United Nations Population Fund	New York
UNHCR	United Nations High Commissioner for Refugees	Geneva
UNICEF	United Nations Children's Fund	New York
UNIDIR	United Nations Institute for Disarmament Research	Geneva
UNIDO	United Nations Industrial Development Organization	Vienna
UNITAR	United Nations Institute for Training and Research	Geneva
UNOPS	United Nations Office for Project Services	Copenhagen
UNRWA	United Nations Relief and Works Agency for Palestine Refugees in the Near East	Amman
UNSSC	United Nations System Staff College	Turin
UNU	United Nations University	Tokyo
UNWTO	World Tourism Organization	Madrid
UPU	Universal Postal Union	Bern
WFP	World Food Programme	Rome
WHO	World Health Organization	Geneva
WIPO	World Intellectual Property Organization	Geneva
WMO	World Meteorological Organization	Geneva
World Bank	World Bank	Washington, DC

NATO MEMBERS

The North Atlantic Treaty Organization (NATO) is a military alliance
founded in 1949 with 12 members. Today, membership of the organisation
runs to the following 30 countries, who joined in the years outlined below.

Year Joined	Country/ies	Year Joined	Country/ies
1949	Belgium, Canada, Denmark, France, Iceland, Italy, Luxembourg, Netherlands, Norway, Portugal, UK, USA	1999	Czech Republic, Hungary, Poland
1952	Greece, Turkey	2004	Bulgaria, Estonia, Latvia, Lithuania, Romania, Slovakia, Slovenia
1955	West Germany (now Germany)	2009	Albania, Croatia
1982	Spain	2017	Montenegro
		2020	North Macedonia

UNASUR

The most successful pan-continental political alliance in South America to
date is UNASUR (South American Union of Nations). This was established
in 2008 with headquarters in Quito, Ecuador, and the following 12
countries as members. Unfortunately, UNASUR has unravelled in recent
years, with most countries suspending or withdrawing their membership.

Argentina · Bolivia · Brazil · Chile · Colombia · Ecuador · Guyana
Paraguay · Peru · Surinam · Uruguay · Venezuela

PRIME MINISTERS OF INDIA

Year	Prime Minister	Year	Prime Minister
1947	Jawaharlal Nehru	1989	VP Singh
1964	Gulzarilal Nanda	1990	Chandra Shekhar
1964	Lal Bahadur Shastri	1991	PV Narasimha Rao
1966	Gulzarilal Nanda	1996	Atal Bihari Vajpayee
1966	Indira Gandhi	1996	HD Deve Gowda
1977	Morarji Desai	1997	Inder Kumar Gujral
1979	Charan Singh	1998	Atal Bihari Vajpayee
1980	Indira Gandhi	2004	Manmohan Singh
1984	Rajiv Gandhi	2014	Narendra Modi

SECRETARIES-GENERAL OF NATO

1952	Hastings Ismay	UK	1994	Willy Claes BE

1952 ....Hastings Ismay UK
1957 .... Paul-Henri Spaak BE
1961 ....Dirk U Stikker NL
1964 .... Manlio Brosio IT
1971 ....Joseph Luns NL
1984 .... Peter Carington UK
1988 .... Manfred Wörner* DE
1994 .... Sergio Balanzino† IT

1994 .... Willy Claes BE
1995 .... Sergio Balanzino† IT
1995 .... Javier Solana ES
1999 .... George Robertson UK
2003 . Alessandro Minuto Rizzo† IT
2004 .... Jaap de Hoop Scheffer NL
2009 .. Anders Fogh Rasmussen DK
2014 .... Jens Stoltenberg NO

* Died in office. † Acting Secretary-General.

COMPULSORY VOTING

Some countries where it is illegal not to vote, although enforcement of the law differs from country to country and penalties for non-compliance vary.

Argentina · Australia · Belgium · Bolivia · Brazil · Bulgaria
DR Congo · Costa Rica · Ecuador · Egypt · Greece · Honduras
Lebanon* · Liechtenstein · Luxembourg · Mexico · Nauru · Panama
Paraguay · Peru · Philippines · Samoa · Singapore · Switzerland†
Thailand · Turkey · Uruguay

* Men aged 21+ only. † Only in one canton (Schaffhausen).

THE G7

Founded in 1975 as the G6, with Canada added in 1976 to make up the current complement, the G7 – or 'Group of Seven' – is an association of the world's leading industrial nations which meet regularly to discuss economic, trade, security and environmental issues. The European Union, while not a member, attends these meetings. From 1998, it was known as the G8, with Russia as the additional member, but, following its invasion of the Crimea in 2014, Russia was suspended and the number of members reduced back to seven. China – despite its growing economic power – has never been a member. The Presidency of the group rotates around the member countries.

Canada · France · Germany · Italy · Japan · UK · USA

THE G20

Beginning in 1999 as a forum for finance ministers and the governors of central banks, the G20 is now an association of advanced and developing economic countries (plus the European Union), representing more than 60 per cent of the world's population. The heads of government of member countries meet at annual summits and the Presidency rotates among them.

Argentina · Australia · Brazil · Canada · China · European Union · France
Germany · India · Indonesia · Italy · Japan · Mexico · Russia · Saudi Arabia
South Africa · South Korea · Turkey · UK · USA

Note: Spain, while not a member, is invited as a permanent guest. Other countries are also invited to join meetings.

RECENT PRIME MINISTERS OF AUSTRALIA

1939	Robert Menzies	1975	Malcolm Fraser
1941	Arthur Fadden	1983	Bob Hawke
1941	John Curtin	1991	Paul Keating
1945	Frank Forde	1996	John Howard
1945	Ben Chifley	2007	Kevin Rudd
1949	Robert Menzies	2010	Julia Gillard
1966	Harold Holt	2013	Kevin Rudd
1967	John McEwen	2013	Tony Abbott
1968	John Gorton	2015	Malcolm Turnbull
1971	William McMahon	2018	Scott Morrison
1972	Gough Whitlam	2022	Anthony Albanese

A REMOVAL FROM OFFICE

Labor's Gough Whitlam secured a unique place in Australian political history in 1975, when he became the only Prime Minister to be removed from office by the Queen's representative, the Governor-General, Sir John Kerr. When Whitlam struggled to pass legislation because of opposition in the Senate, and declined to call a new election, Kerr dismissed him and installed a caretaker Government under the Liberal leader Malcolm Fraser.*

* Letters released in 2020 reveal that the Queen was not given prior warning.

143

RECENT PRIME MINISTERS OF NEW ZEALAND

1935	Michael Joseph Savage	1975	Robert Muldoon
1940	Peter Fraser	1984	David Lange
1949	Sidney Holland	1989	Geoffrey Palmer
1957	Keith Holyoake	1990	Mike Moore
1957	Walter Nash	1990	James Bolger
1960	Keith Holyoake	1997	Jenny Shipley
1972	John Marshall	1999	Helen Clark
1972	Norman Kirk	2008	John Key
1974	Hugh Watt*	2016	Bill English
1974	Bill Rowling	2017	Jacinda Ardern

* Acting Prime Minister.

AUSTRALIA'S WOMAN PRIME MINISTER

Julia Gillard became the first (and so far only) woman to be Prime Minister of Australia when, in 2010, she replaced the incumbent, Kevin Rudd, as leader of the Australian Labor Party. Gillard – born in Barry, Wales in 1961 – is one of eight Australian Prime Ministers not to be born in the country.

CARICOM

Founded in 1973, the Caribbean Community (CARICOM) is an association of 15 countries, plus five associate members, covering an area from the Bahamas to Suriname and Guyana in South America. The body exists to improve economic integration, security, social development and the coordination of foreign policy, with headquarters in Georgetown, Guyana.

Year Joined	Country/ies	Year Joined	Country/ies
1973	Barbados, Guyana, Jamaica, Trinidad and Tobago		St Kitts and Nevis, St Vincent and the Grenadines
1974	Antigua and Barbuda, Belize, Dominica, Grenada, Montserrat, St Lucia,	1983	Bahamas
		1995	Suriname
		2002	Haiti

Note: Associate members are Anguilla, Bermuda, British Virgin Islands, Cayman Islands and Turks and Caicos Islands.

THE PARLIAMENT OF CANADA

The home of Canada's Parliament is Parliament Hill in the national capital, Ottawa. The building was constructed from 1859 in Gothic Revival style (inspired by the Palace of Westminster in London), overlooking the Ottawa River, and was officially opened in 1866. A fire in 1916 claimed seven lives and destroyed the central block, where Parliament actually met. This was then rebuilt using modern materials to try to reflect the original structure.

RECENT PRIME MINISTERS OF JAPAN

1939 .... Nobuyuki Abe	1982 .... Yasuhiro Nakasone
1940 ....Mitsumasa Yonai	1987 .... Noboru Takeshita
1940 ....Fumimaro Konoe	1989 ....Sōsuke Uno
1941 .... Hideki Tōjō	1989 .... Toshiki Kaifu
1944 ....Kuniaki Koiso	1991 .... Kiichi Miyazawa
1945 ....Kantarō Suzuki	1993 .... Morihiro Hosokawa
1945 .... Naruhiko Higashikuni	1994 .... Tsutomu Hata
1945 .... Kijūrō Shidehara	1994 .... Tomiichi Murayama
1946 .... Shigeru Yoshida	1996 .... Ryūtarō Hashimoto
1947 .... Tetsu Katayama	1998 ....Keizō Obuchi
1948 .... Hitoshi Ashida	2000 ....Yoshirō Mori
1948 .... Shigeru Yoshida	2001 .... Junichirō Koizumi
1954 .... Ichirō Hatoyama	2006 ....Shinzō Abe
1956 .... Tanzan Ishibashi	2007 .... Yasuo Fukuda
1957 ....Nobusuke Kishi	2008 .... Tarō Asō
1960 ....Hayato Ikeda	2009 ....Yukio Hatoyama
1964 ....Eisaku Satō	2010 ....Naoto Kan
1972 ....Kakuei Tanaka	2011 ....Yoshihiko Noda
1974 ....Takeo Miki	2012 ....Shinzō Abe
1976 .... Takeo Fukuda	2020 .... Yoshihide Suga
1978 ....Masayoshi Ōhira	2021 ....Fumio Kishida
1980 ....Zenkō Suzuki	

THE ARAB SPRING

The Arab Spring series of pro-democracy uprisings across Africa and the Middle East began in Tunisia in 2010 and, with only partial success, spread to other countries, most notably Egypt, Yemen, Bahrain, Libya and Syria.

THE UNITED ARAB EMIRATES

Abu Dhabi · Ajman · Dubai · Fujairah · Ras Al Khaimah
Sharjah · Umm Al Quwain

THE FIRST WOMEN PRIME MINISTERS
OUTSIDE EUROPE

Country	Prime Minister	Year
Australia	Julia Gillard	2010
Bangladesh	Khaleda Zia	1991
Barbados	Mia Mottley	2018
Bermuda	Pamela Gordon-Banks	1997
Burundi	Sylvie Kinigi	1993
Canada	Kim Campbell	1993
Central African Republic	Elisabeth Domitien	1975
Dominica	Eugenia Charles	1980
Gabon	Rose Christiane Raponda	2020
Haiti	Claudette Werleigh	1995
India	Indira Gandhi	1966
Israel	Golda Meir	1969
Jamaica	Portia Simpson-Miller	2006
Mali	Cissé Mariam Kaïdama Sidibé	2011
Mozambique	Luísa Dia Dogo	2004
Namibia	Saara Kuugongelwa-Amadhila	2015
Netherlands Antilles	Lucina da Costa Gomez-Matheeuws	1977
New Zealand	Jenny Shipley	1997
Pakistan	Benazir Bhutto	1988
Peru	Beatriz Merino	2003
Rwanda	Agathe Uwilingiyimana	1993
Samoa	Fiamē Naomi Mataʻafa	2021
São Tomé and Principe	Maria das Neves	2002
Senegal	Mame Madior Boye	2001
Sri Lanka*	Sirimavo Bandaranaike†	1960
Thailand	Yingluck Shinawatra	2011
Togo	Victoire Tomegah Dogbé	2020
Trinidad and Tobago	Kamla Persad-Bissessar	2010
Tunisia	Najla Bouden	2021

* Then Ceylon. † The world's first woman Prime Minister.

PRESIDENTS OF SOUTH AFRICA

1961	Charles Robberts Swart	1984	Pieter Willem ('PW') Botha
1967	Jozua ('Tom') Naude*	1989	Chris Heunis*
1968	Jacobus ('Jim') Fouché	1989	Frederik Willem ('FW') de Klerk
1975	Johannes de Klerk*	1994	Nelson Mandela
1975	Nicolaas Diederichs	1999	Thabo Mbeki
1978	Marais Viljoen*	2008	Kgalema Motlanthe
1978	Balthazar ('John') Vorster	2009	Jacob Zuma
1979	Marais Viljoen	2018	Cyril Ramaphosa

* Acting President.

Note: From 1961 to 1984, the office was known as State President of the Republic and the position was largely ceremonial. In 1984, the title was changed to President of the Republic and the office became more politically powerful, coinciding with the abolition of the post of Prime Minister.

THE AUSTRALIAN PARLIAMENT

Australia's legislature meets in the national capital, Canberra. Parliament moved there from Melbourne in 1927, taking up residence in what was meant to be a temporary building, but remained in service for 61 years. A new home – Parliament House on Capital Hill – finally opened in 1988, following eight years of construction. Internally, the decorative colours of the two Chambers echo the colours used in the Houses of Parliament in the UK – green for the House of Representatives and red for the Senate.

ASEAN

The Association of Southeast Asian Nations (ASEAN) was founded in 1967 to foster peace and economic and cultural ties among its (now ten) member countries, who joined the organisation in the years listed below. Since 1976, administration has been handled by a secretariat based in Jakarta, Indonesia.

Year Joined	Country/ies	Year Joined	Country/ies
1967	Indonesia, Malaysia, Philippines, Singapore, Thailand	1995	Vietnam
		1997	Laos, Myanmar
1984	Brunei	1999	Cambodia

OFFICIAL LANGUAGES OF THE UNITED NATIONS

Arabic · Chinese · English · French · Russian · Spanish

THE COMMONWEALTH

The Commonwealth – an association of 56 sovereign states – has its roots in the British Commonwealth of Nations, established in 1926 to confirm that the United Kingdom and its increasingly independent overseas dominions were equal members of a community within the British Empire. Other countries joined the organisation after gaining independence from the UK, but membership today is not confined to former Empire countries.

Year Joined	Country/ies
1926	UK
1931	Australia, Canada, New Zealand, South Africa*
1947	India, Pakistan†
1948	Sri Lanka
1957	Ghana, Malaysia
1960	Cameroon, Nigeria‡
1961	Cyprus, Sierra Leone, Tanzania
1962	Jamaica, Trinidad and Tobago, Uganda
1963	Kenya
1964	Malawi, Malta, Zambia
1965	The Gambia§, Singapore
1966	Barbados, Botswana Guyana, Lesotho
1968	Eswatini, Mauritius
1970	Fiji¶, Samoa, Tonga
1972	Bangladesh
1973	The Bahamas
1974	Grenada
1975	Papua New Guinea
1976	Seychelles
1978	Dominica, Solomon Islands, Tuvalu
1979	Kiribati, St Lucia, St Vincent and the Grenadines
1980	Vanuatu
1981	Antigua and Barbuda, Belize
1982	Maldives#
1983	St Kitts and Nevis
1984	Brunei
1990	Namibia
1995	Mozambique**
1999	Nauru††
2009	Rwanda**
2022	Gabon, Togo**

* Left in 1961 but rejoined in 1994. † Left in 1972 but rejoined in 1989.

‡ Membership suspended 1995–99. § Left in 2013 but rejoined in 2018.

¶ Membership suspended 1987–97, 2000–01 and 2006–14.

Left in 2016 but rejoined in 2020.

** Country with no historic ties to the UK.

†† Associate member from 1968.

SECRETARIES-GENERAL OF THE UNITED NATIONS

1946–52.....................Trygve Lie NO	1992–96.. Boutros Boutros-Ghali EG
1953–61...... Dag Hammarskjöld SE	1997–2006 .... Kofi Annan GH
1962–71......................U Thant* MM	2007–16................Ban Ki-Moon KR
1972–81.............Kurt Waldheim AT	2017–............. António Guterres PT
1982–91 ..Javier Pérez de Cuéllar PE	

* Initially Acting Secretary-General from 1961 after the death of
Dag Hammarskjöld in a plane crash.

AUSTRALIA'S ELECTION WINNERS

Australia has a track record of changing its Prime Minister between general elections with the result that only the following nine of the 31 office holders to date actually won an election to become Prime Minister for the first time.

Joseph Cook · James Scullin · Joseph Lyons · Gough Whitlam · Bob Hawke
John Howard · Kevin Rudd · Tony Abbott · Anthony Albanese

RECENT PRIME MINISTERS OF CANADA

1935 .... William Mackenzie King	1984 .... John Turner
1948 ....Louis St Laurent	1984 ....Brian Mulroney
1957 ....John Diefenbaker	1993 ....Kim Campbell
1963 ....Lester Pearson	1993 ....Jean Chrétien
1968 .... Pierre Trudeau	2003 ....Paul Martin
1979 .... Joe Clark	2006 ....Stephen Harper
1980 .... Pierre Trudeau	2015 ....Justin Trudeau

THE GREAT HALL OF THE PEOPLE

The National People's Congress, comprising nearly 3,000 members, is China's most important legislative body, with the power to change the Constitution, appoint leading officials and approve and enact key legislation. The Congress meets once annually, for approximately a couple of weeks, and the venue is the Great Hall of the People, a vast, colonnaded structure that opened on the western side of Tiananmen Square in Beijing in 1959.

SOME BICAMERAL PARLIAMENTS OF THE WORLD

Country	Parliament	Lower Chamber	Upper Chamber
Argentina	Congreso de la Nacion	Cámara de Diputados	Senado
Australia	Parliament	House of Representatives	Senate
Austria	Bundesversammlung	Nationalrat	Bundesrat
Belgium	Parlement fédéral/ Federaal Parlement	Chambre des Représentants/Kamer van Volksvertenwoordigers	Sénat/Senaat
Brazil	Congreso Nacional	Câmara dos Deputados	Senado Federal
Canada	Parliament/ Parlement	House of Commons/ Chambre des communes	Senate/Sénat
Czech Rep.	Parlament	Poslanecká sněmovna	Senát
Egypt	Parliament	Majlis Al-Nowaab	Majlis Al-Shiyoukh
France	Parlement	Assemblée nationale	Sénat
Germany	Parlament	Bundestag	Bundesrat
India	Sansad	Lok Sabha	Rajya Sabha
Ireland	Oireachtas	Dáil Éireann	Seanad Éireann
Isle of Man	Tynwald	House of Keys	Legislative Council
Italy	Parlamento	Camera dei Deputati	Senato della Repubblica
Japan	Diet/Kokkai	Shūgiin	Sangiin
Mexico	Congreso de la Unión	Cámara de Diputados	Cámara de Senadores
Netherlands	Staten-Generaal	Tweede Kamer	Eerste Kamer
Oman	Majlis Oman	Majlis al-Shura	Majlis al-Dalwa
Pakistan	Parliament	National Assembly	Senate
Poland	Zgromadzenie Narodowe	Sejm	Senat
Russia	Federalnoye Sobraniye	Gosudarstvennaya Duma	Sovet Federatsii
Slovenia	Državni zbor	Državni zbor	Državni svet
Spain	Cortes Generales	Congreso de los Diputados	Senado
S Africa	Parliament	National Assembly	National Council of Provinces
UK	Parliament	House of Commons	House of Lords
USA	Congress	House of Representatives	Senate
Zimbabwe	Parliament	National Assembly	Senate

SOME UNICAMERAL PARLIAMENTS OF THE WORLD

Country	Parliament
Bulgaria	Narodno Sabranie
China	Quanguo Renmin Daibiao Dahui (National People's Congress)
Croatia	Hrvatski sabor
Cuba	Asamblea Nacional del Poder Popular
Cyprus	House of Representatives/ Vouli Antiprosopon
Denmark	Folketing
Estonia	Riigikogu
Finland	Eduskunta
Hungary	Országgyűlés
Iceland	Alþingi
Iran	Majles Shoraye Eslami
Israel	Knesset
Monaco	Conseil National
New Zealand	Parliament (House of Representatives)
Norway	Storting
Portugal	Assembleia da República
San Marino	Consiglio Grande e Generale
Sweden	Riksdag

FIRST LADY – FOR THE SECOND TIME

When Graça Machel married South Africa's Nelson Mandela, it was her second marriage to the President of a country. Machel, born Graça Simbine, was initially the wife of Samora Machel – the first President of the newly-independent Mozambique – from 1975 until his death in 1986. Twelve years later, she married Mandela and became a 'first lady' for the second time – a fact that sadly tends to overshadow her own considerable, internationally-recognised work as a teacher and human rights campaigner.

NICKNAMES OF WORLD LEADERS

Aunty Helen	Helen Clark	NZ
Baby Doc	Jean-Claude Duvalier	HT
Bibi	Benjamin Netanyahu	IL
Big Crocodile	PW Botha	ZA
Bongbong	Ferdinand Marcos Jr	PH
Bulldozer	Ariel Sharon	IL
Butternut	Jacob Zuma	ZA
Clever Chameleon	FW de Klerk	ZA
Cupcake	Cyril Ramaphosa	ZA
El Caballo	Fidel Castro	CU
Lizard of Oz	Paul Keating	AU
Mad Monk	Tony Abbott	AU
Madiba	Nelson Mandela	ZA
Mahatma	Mohandas Gandhi	IN
Mother India	Indira Gandhi	IN
NaMo	Narendra Modi	IN
Old Man	David Ben-Gurion	IL
Papa Doc	François Duvalier	HT
Pet	Pierre Trudeau	CA
Silver Bodgie	Bob Hawke	AU
Toby Tosspot	Edmund Barton	AU
Uncle Bob	Robert Mugabe	ZW

151

PRIME MINISTERS OF ISRAEL

1948 ....David Ben-Gurion	1986 ....Yitzhak Shamir
1954 ....Moshe Sharett	1992 .... Yitzhak Rabin
1955 ....David Ben-Gurion	1995 ....Shimon Peres
1963 .... Levi Eshkol	1996 ....Benjamin Netanyahu
1969 .... Yigal Allon*	1999 .... Ehud Barak
1969 ....Golda Meir	2001 ....Ariel Sharon
1974 .... Yitzhak Rabin	2006 ....Ehud Olmert
1977 .... Menachem Begin	2009 ....Benjamin Netanyahu
1983 ....Yitzhak Shamir	2021 .... Naftali Bennett
1984 ....Shimon Peres	2022 ....Yair Lapid

* Acting Prime Minister.

THE ORIGINAL GANG OF FOUR

Four hard-line members of the Chinese Communist Party in the 1960s, who were close associates of Party Chairman Mao Zedong, became infamous for the power they yielded and their control of the media. After Mao's death, all four were tried and convicted of an attempt to seize power.

Jiang Qing* · Wang Hongwen · Zhang Chunqiao · Yao Wenyuan

* Third wife of Mao Zedong.

'OCRACIES'

There are numerous alternative ways in which a country might be governed.

'Ocracy'	Ruled By	'Ocracy'	Ruled By
Aristocracy ....Nobility		Kleptocracy ....Corrupt officials	
Autocracy .... One person		Meritocracy .... Talented people	
Democracy .... People		Ochlocracy ....Mob	
Ergatocracy.......................... Workers		Plutocracy..............................Wealthy	
Gerontocracy .... Old people		Stratocracy.............................Military	
Gynaecocracy....................... Women		Technocracy .... Experts	
Hierocracy............................... Clergy		Theocracy................................ Clergy	
Kakistocracy.............. Worst citizens		Timocracy ....Property owners	

THE ARAB LEAGUE

The Arab League, or the League of Arab States, was set up in Cairo in 1945 to strengthen economic, political, cultural and social ties between countries.

Year Joined	Country/ies	Year Joined	Country/ies
1945	Egypt*, Iraq, Jordan, Lebanon, Saudi Arabia, Syria†, Yemen	1971	Bahrain, Oman, Qatar, United Arab Emirates
1953	Libya‡	1973	Mauritania
1956	Sudan	1974	Somalia
1958	Morocco, Tunisia	1976	Palestine§
1961	Kuwait	1977	Djibouti
1962	Algeria	1993	Comoros

* Suspended 1979–89. † Suspended in 2011.
‡ Suspended briefly in 2011. § Initially as the Palestine Liberation Organization.

NEW ZEALAND'S WOMEN RECORD BREAKERS

When Jacinda Ardern was sworn into office in 2017, she became New Zealand's youngest ever Prime Minister (aged 37). When her daughter was born in 2018, she also became only the second international leader to give birth in office – after Benazir Bhutto of Pakistan in 1990. Ardern wasn't New Zealand's first woman Prime Minister, however. That honour goes to Jenny Shipley who took office in 1997, just ahead of Helen Clark in 1999.

THE BLUE HOUSE

America may have the White House but in South Korea the most prestigious political property is blue. From the foundation of the country in 1948 until 2022, the Blue House, located in parkland in a suburb of the capital Seoul, was the mysterious home of the President. Constructed by Japan during its colonial rule, the secluded pavilion-like structure with its distinctive blue roof tiles was heavily guarded and out of reach of citizens. However, in May 2022, the newly-elected President Yoon Suk-yeol moved the Presidential residence to the defence ministry a few miles away and threw open the complex and its mountainside grounds to the public. Now up to 39,000 curious people a day visit these once strictly-private premises.

INDEX